The Language of Light

Mind-drawing from the Higher Self
By
Nadine May

Published by:
Kima Global Publishers
50 Clovelly road, Clovelly 7975
P.O. Box 22404 Fish Hook
Cape Town
South Africa

Contact Details:

Publisher: info@kimaglobal.co.za
Website: http://www.kimaglobal.co.za

Author: nadinemay@global.co.za
Website: http://www.ascensiontopics.com

© Nadine May 2001
ISBN: 978-0-9814278-5-0

All rights reserved. With the exception of small passages quoted for review purposes, no portion of this work may be reproduced, translated, adapted, stored in a retrieval system, or transmitted in any form or through any means including electronic, mechanical, photocopying or otherwise without the written permission of the publisher.

First edition: April 2003
Second edition July 2009
Cover Art and illustrations by Author Nadine May

Other books by Nadine May

Meditations on the Language of Light
The Awakening Clan
The Astral Explorer
The Cosmic Traveller
<u>Forthcoming:</u> 2010
  Vanishing Worlds
  The Body Codes on Light

Dedication

This book is dedicated to two friends Henk and Maria who both made a big difference to my life through knowing them. Although both never met each other in the flesh, I know these words will reach them.

Maria, you packed such Language of Light qualities into the time we spent together while enduring so much pain, and you could still express a sense of humour through it all. I heard your laughter while meditating and knew then that you had left our world. It told me that my work had truly begun.

Dearest Henk, you inspired me through your creativity to complete this workbook and the words written in the sand "You are my idea. One day you will look for me and I'll be gone" reminded me of your sudden departure. Through these words I truly say goodbye until we meet again.

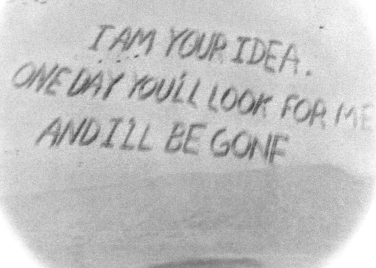

Acknowledgments

The words I am looking for to express my gratitude to Robin are not in the English dictionary. They are written in my heart.

How grateful am I to have found a friend, a companion and soul mate that so willingly gave me full support in order to finish this workbook. He even took my workload from me so I could devote my time to completing it.

Robin a special thanks for the moment, when everything went wrong due to the lack of virtual memory, when you ordered more ram for my PC. Thanks also for the continuous supply of meals, tea, coffee and extras...

My dearest Frances Charles, I thank you for the week you spent with us while proof reading this workbook. You are truly an angel in human guise.

A great thanks to all my students who so enthusiastically followed me without knowing where I would take them. Without you there would have been no workbook. They understood that self-realization is not something one can learn from books, it comes only through personal experience. That is why this workbook was created, so it would become a meditative tool in order to reconnect with the artist's innate wisdom.

Although the workbook requires that students make their own Language of Light symbols so that they become personal, (in order to decode their own genetic codes in Annelies' workbook titled 'Our Body Codes of Light')the symbols in this book were derived from those used by the Spiritual School of Ascension.

I am grateful for their inspiration. They are universal symbols that carry no copyright. *Nadine May*

6 The Language of Light

Contents

Dedication	4
Acknowledgments	5
Foreword	10
Preface	12
Introduction	14
What do the words Art-analogue-Symbolism mean?	14
The Power of the Spoken Word	16
The Power behind the Language of Light	17
The Law of Electromagnetism	18
The Law of the Gift of our Free Will	19
The Law of Space - Time	20
The Five Processes of our four lower bodies through which we Manifest our Reality	22
The Five Stages of Creativity	23
An Art-analogue introduction	30
✎ The Tools you Need	32

The First Stage - Starts with having an idea

Welcome to your Art-analogue-symbolism workshop	34
The Seven Psychic Centres	37
Any Creation starts with an Idea	38
• First exercise on a mundane level	38
• First exercise on a soul level	39
Your Psychic Feeling centres are:	40
We are all Psychics!	40
• Second exercise on a mundane level	40
• Second exercise on a soul level	41
Our Psychic Hearing centres are:	42
• Third exercise on a mundane level	42
• Third exercise on a soul level	43
Our Psychic Intuitive/Creative centre	44
• Fourth exercise on a mundane level	44
• Fourth exercise on a soul level	45
Your twelve life style focussed doodles	47
• Any thought that <u>influences</u> your Conscious mind	49
• Any thought is <u>stored</u> by your Conscious mind	51
• Any quality that <u>inspires</u> your Conscious mind	53
• Any <u>Idea</u> that will <u>inspire</u> your Conscious mind	55
The **1st** Language of Light Quality	58
✎ Your Language of Light Card of <u>Forgiveness</u>	59
The **Base Chakra**: your instinctual mind channel	60
• With the symbol of Forgiveness	60

Flower of Life Stage

Fruit of Life Stage

Your First insight

The Second Stage - Ideas are investigated

Your Logical and Literal Mind. 68
- Where your ideas are investigated. 68

The Mandala of your Emotional Expressions. 70
Your **2nd** Language of Light Quality 72
- Your Language of Light Card of <u>Structure</u> 73

The **Sacral Chakra**: our emotional intelligence. 74
- With your symbol of Structure 74

Your Second insight

The Third Stage - Where ideas are explored through action

The Nine Masks You Wear. 82
Your **3rd** Language of Light Quality 84
- Your symbol of Inner Power 84

Your Language of Light Card of <u>Inner Power</u> 85
The **Solar Plexus**: your questioning mind. 86
The Perception we have of Ourselves 88
Your Body Language. 90
Your **4th** Language of Light Quality 96
- Your symbol for Compassion 96

Your Language of Light Card of <u>Compassion</u>. 97
The **Heart Chakra**: your holistic mind channel 98

Your Third insight

The Fourth Stage - Where ideas start to manifest

Your Fourth pathway of the Soul. 105
Your Nine gifts that can enrich this reality 106
Colour and your Senses. 108
Your **5th** Language of Light Quality 112
- Your Language of Light Card of the <u>Breath of Life</u> 113

The **Throat Chakra**: your abundance channel 114
- With the symbol of the Breath of life. 114

Honour your Divine Within 116

Your Fourth insight

The Fifth Stage - Where ideas are manifested

The Fifth pathway for your soul 123
The Sound of Your name. 124
The first Melody you heard 125
The **6th** Language of Light Quality 128
- Your Language of Light Card of <u>Unconditional Love</u>. 129

Star Tetrahedron

Metatron's Cube

Cube

Octahedron

Icosahedron

Fruit of Life

8 The Language of Light

The **Third Eye Chakra**: your Higher mind channel 130
  • With the symbol of Unconditional Love 130
Your Mandala is a reflection of your real self 132
Your **7th** Language of Light Quality 134
  • Is the symbol of Freedom 134
  ✎ Your Language of Light Card of <u>Freedom</u> 135
The vibration of your Third Eye energy field 136
The **Crown Chakra**: your cosmic awareness mind 138
The vibration level of your Etheric energy field 140
The Auric field of your Soul body 142

Your Fifth insight

Our Light Body

We are all Energy Beings 151
Our Ascension into a new Paradigm 152
Elemental Alchemy 154
Colour, Shape and our Senses 155
The 48 Universal Language of Light symbols 156
Our Original Blueprint 158
Your Five Observation points 159
Your Five Elemental cards 161
The **10th** Language of Light Quality 164
  ✎ Your Language of Light Card of <u>Peaceful Bliss</u> 165
Body awareness through the element of Earth 166
  ✎ Your Earth Power card 167
The **11 th** Language of Light Quality 170
  ✎ Your Language of Light Card of <u>Direction</u> 171
Body awareness through the element of Water 172
  ✎ Your Water Power card 173
The **12 th** Language of Light Quality 176
  ✎ Your Language of Light Card of <u>Hope</u> 177
Body awareness through the element of Fire 178
  ✎ Your Fire Power card 179
The **13 th** Language of Light Quality 182
  ✎ Your Language of Light Card of <u>Divine Union</u> 183
Body awareness through the element of Air 184
  ✎ Your Air Power card 185
The **14th** Language of Light Quality 188
  ✎ Your Language of Light Card of <u>Abundance</u> 189
Body awareness through the element of Ether 190
  ✎ Your Ether Power card 191

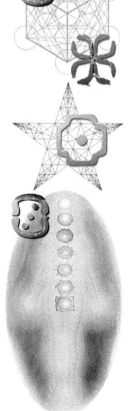

Closure 192

Interpretations

Welcome to your workshop page............................ 196
The Seven Centres of Consciousness 198
Your body symptoms on the <u>First level</u> of awakening.. 200
The Red, Yellow and Green colour energies in your drawings........ 203
- Your Hidden Symbols in Red 205
- The Yellow energies in your drawing.............. 206
- Your Hidden Symbols in Yellow 207
- Your Hidden Symbols in Green 209

What is revealed through your doodles?................... 210
Your Doodles in Depth 214
Your body symptoms on the <u>Second level</u> of awakening.. 218
The Orange and Blue energy in Your drawings 220
- The Hidden symbols in Orange.................... 221
- The Blue energy in your drawings 223
- The Hidden Symbols in Blue...................... 224

Your Body Language....................................... 226
Your body symptoms on the <u>Third level</u> of awakening............ 228
Your Violet/ Indigo energy through your drawings......... 229
- Your Hidden Symbols in Violet/ Indigo 230

The Language of Colour 231
Colour has two divisions: 232
Awakening through the Etheric levels.................... 237
Your body symptoms through the <u>Fourth level</u> of awakening 238
The Magenta/Violet energy through our drawings........... 239
- The Hidden Symbols of Magenta................... 241

Your body symptoms during the <u>Fifth level</u> of Awakening........ 242
Salute to the Sun 243
The Booklet is used for your The Body Codes of Light 245
The Law of Karma 246
The Creation of our World............................... 247
Your Chakra cards 248
Your dream Home example 249

Your booklet instructions - for the Awakening Game

Index/Glossary 260
Bibliography... 267
About the Author 269

Foreword

My first experience with Nadine's Art-analogue mind drawing workshop in 2002 was a revelation. The idea that one can access one's unconscious thought processes by simply doodling, was new to me. The effect of the different exercises all accompanied by soothing music was magical in terms of moving me out of a linear mind set. It truly helped to open the door to my imagination.

When I took a peek at the artworks on the walls, I realised that there was no right or wrong way, just our own individual way. That was such a relief, since I do not regard myself as an artist.

It turns out that our daydreaming doodles can expand our infinite awesomeness, not only to help with our daily tasks, but also to help us to remember what goes on during meetings or phone conversations. That's why people, myself included, doodle when on the phone.

I found that out much later, when I was trying to listen to someone's promotional talk over the phone. In the past I could easily have allowed the other person to persuade me to agree with them. As I was doodling, and later looked at what I had drawn, I could see that a part of me had a different opinion regarding the conversation, and did not agree at all.

A few years ago I was involved in researching how people learn and found this subject to be very well documented. The key to Nadine's work reminded me what I had read up about how we learn, or accumulate information. You have to be active by touching the object and moving your hands. Nadine has proven that doodling takes the place of actually putting your hands on the topic at hand thus focussing our attention.

Males tend to be kinetic learners and part of the reason they have such a hard time in schools these days must have something to do with how their hands and fingers connect with their brains. I wish now that my younger son who had a hard time in school, had had the opportunity of attending Nadine's class. It would have made a huge difference.

I was certainly not observing my art work piece consciously, but the similarity of my finished doodle drawings to those appearing in Nadine's workbook reinforced my sense of how the unconscious mind is part of our conscious behaviour, rather than in a Jungian sense a separate closed compartment which can only be opened with conscious effort.

I became aware that by exploring our creative power through doodling, thus releasing our imagination, it is possible to use one's intent to attract into our life our most exciting dreams and desires. This special way of doodling is such an innocent yet powerful tool that it becomes an essential part of life.

The first publication was a great success We received reviews and sales from all over the world. Thus encouraged the book has gone to a second edition.

Robin Beck (Publisher)

Reviews on the The language of Light

This unusual workbook is one of a kind. I was rivetted by the explanation of the Language of Light. The many illustrations and creative formats that help one to create their own Language of Light cards, is phenomenal. This workbook is a breakthrough from the point of bringing into perspective how each one of us can embody more psychic energy.

The mind-drawing activities with each exercise are creative meditations.

I have used some of the exercises in my own workshops and they truly work

Sue Barker, Academy for Art Therapy & The Power of the Mind – Paarl, Western Cape

This amazing book further develops the Language of Light mentioned in Nadine's novel "The Awakening Clan". Using the Techniques of Mind Drawing, the reader is connected with their own intuitive nature, the Language of their Soul. This is a workbook which explains the Chakra system, how it resonates with your thought patterns and how emotional patterns are established, which affect your later life. Beautifully produced and easy to use, this book is most recommended.

Renaissance Magazine June 2003

The Meditation Language of Light book

Having enjoyed the idea behind Nadine's creative unusual meditation exercises, I visited her website and was even more surprised at this author's effort to bring controversial topics to the general public. And all her articles are for Free! I have applied her idea to use a creative meditation exercises that the Language of Light workbook offers and practised her meditation technics for myself. Congratulations.

John Bishop (spiritual counsellor. UK)

The "exercises" in Meditations on the Language of Light have opened me up in a manner that is new to me. I haven't coloured anything in in SUCH a long long time, that at first I was worried about it being perfect and was rather stiff, then as I moved on, I let go and I was a child again, full of imagination and creativity - and I'm having so much fun!! In "the rest of my life" things also began to change, well the way I looked at things began to change. I was less stiff and precise in the way things had to be, I opened up and started seeing things with "new eyes", I noticed that I was smiling a lot more often and actually LAUGHING and really feeling it, the scowl was left behind with the stiffness. I haven't finished the book yet, but I'm working on it......I'm definitely working on it!!

Monica Pinto - Artist and teacher of Art

Preface

We all know that any language we use is a medium through which we exchange our thoughts, be it in a written, verbal or mental telepathy form. But where is the observer?

Our forefathers all used a language that belonged to their time. The principles of speech have evolved over long periods. Even the Neanderthal Man could speak. Writing must have developed later. First they became pictorial symbols and later they became the written word. The idea of materializing concepts into actualities by the medium of the word (or idea) was the origin of this creation!

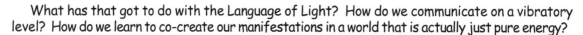

If this creation is 'like a dream' and the power of the word was the fundamental principle of the power of magic, writing is then probably one of the the greatest inventions in human history.

What has that got to do with the Language of Light? How do we communicate on a vibratory level? How do we learn to co-create our manifestations in a world that is actually just pure energy?

These are some of the questions I kept asking myself during the time that the mind-drawing exercises started to replace my drawing skill techniques. Teaching how to learn the skill of drawing the pictorial image we see around us, I was guided to find a way how to draw the energy that creates those physical images. What energy is it that keeps our dream world vibrating at a slow pace in order to manifest physical matter? Who is the observer of our global human community?

How many other worlds are there out there vibrating at a different speed so that only during our dream time are we aware of them? Could it be possible that we can snap out of this 3rd dimensional dream world into a 5th dimensional dream world at a blink of an eye? Could the secret to immortality be hidden in our Mother Tongue?

I kept hearing that the answer was YES, providing we don't consume all our energy in keeping this illusion alive, but that we learn to tap into universal energy that is stored in our body of light. We are all pure energy, we are beings of light. This workbook is all about how we tap into this DIVINE ENERGY to...

Discover the Language of Light that activates our Body of Light.

If we perceive that our 'soul' body is an auric energy field then the Vital Life Force (spirit) must be the 'driver' behind this energy field. Without this vital life force (spirit) there can be no Soul because our Soul is an energy-expression of all our spiritual experiences. Our soul is like a library. Let's call this library our aura that holds our akashic records. So what would it take in order to read the books in our soul library? What language would be used by the soul? Any thought we have must be accompanied by a feeling if we want to manifest anything. We voice millions of words every day but only if our thoughts are accompanied by feelings, only then does our soul absorb those words. That energy becomes like a mirror. This mirror, or dream, is the world we live in. Our daily experiences are a reflection of the feelings we think, write down or utter.

Our every thought, if it is accompanied by a feeling, is stored or filed away as an experience. It's the feeling we give any thought that matters. That keeps us in the dream.

Everyone can have access to their inner wisdom. I know that every living soul that has chosen to embody a physical vehicle in our special times, had a reason for doing so. Some choose to awaken from this third dimensional dream. Being alive means that I can experience anything I like. I AM the main driver or observer of the dream I co-created. I can awaken from the dream and gain back the freedom to project my consciousness into other dream worlds, but for this I need energy!

My soul has all the energy for that goal, but it only projects between 5 —10% of its energy through each embodiment. The more energy I, the observer, can bring into this dream experience the better the chances are that I can snap out of this illusion in the blink of an eye.

In order to awaken the wisdom of the soul <u>through</u> a physical embodiment, there has to be some clearing of distorted programs that keep this world of illusion intact. It's through our feeling nature that our soul is motivated by our spiritual force to embody more of itself.

The art-analogue mind-drawing exercises were inspired through my drawing skill classes, which I held for many years.

It's through the character 'named Tieneke' in my novel: '**The Awakening Clan**', that this mind-drawing-book became alive. Her thoughts became mine. I'm the observer of her dreamworld. It always astounded me how easy it is for me to look at our physical world through others. By 'others' I mean the characters in my novel called; Ingrid, Annelies, Richard, Tieneke and many more that partake in a genetic decoding workshop in order to awaken the initiate within to reach full consciousness.

Tieneke explores how each one can create a tool that will awaken a doorway or channel into other worlds or realms beyond this limited earthly one.

Each of us have many Language of Light qualities that ,when embodied, would expand our energy body in order to create a more harmonious reality in this dimension. In order to bring more aspects of our soul into our daily lives, we need to open our soul-library and draw in the wisdom through the qualities of the Language of Light. Those qualities will enrich and transform us and our body,our biological cellular expression of consciousness, and free us from this dream world, this third dimensional illusion we call reality.

Nadine May April 2003

Introduction

What do the words Art-analogue-Symbolism mean?

Welcome to my introduction class, I'm Tieneke who for the rest of your mind-drawing course will share all my experiences with you as an art-energy therapy teacher.

The word **ART** reflects a creative quality through any media that integrates human skills, aptitude, or a knack in order to bring into visual representation the thinking process of our Real Self within.

Art-analogue is a mind drawing technique that extracts information from your akashic records, into your reality awareness. We interpret our visual thinking mode through doodling, colour and pictorial or symbolic images. Any creative expression comes from our soul.

Symbolism is the language of our inner or third eye. Our ancestors often expressed their earthly experiences through symbols. The beautiful hieroglyphs inside ancient temples, like those in Egypt are a good example. We can once again learn to express our ideas and emotions through pictorial symbols and learn the interpretations of them. We all know that one picture can express a thousand words.

I will share with you what I feel it means to awaken to full consciousness. It took a while before I could truly accept the possibility myself. Annelies repeatedly mentioned that POWAH, a guide, often spoke about the Language of Light, but only when I learned to travel inter-dimensionally and started to remember my dreams, was I ready to fully grasp what the dynamic of the Language of Light was all about. I speculate that it is our original mother tongue gong back say 200.000 years ago. POWAH often called me Nidaba, (the goddess of writing)

When we started to work together it was POWAH who communicated to me through my analogue drawings. It was uncanny at first. As the moving images flashed before my eyes, the brilliant colours that pulsated from these symbols triggered every fibre in my body. As I started to work with them, the feelings that came with each symbol prepared me for my soul's journey through the seven chakras into inner space.

Throughout this workbook many readers will again start to think in colour, symbols and pictures instead of just words. Every creative expression has a certain energy. Due to their personal interaction with the energy from their drawings, quite a few of my students were contacted on an inner plane and ended up in Annelies' genetic decoding workshops.

Some of my readers will have already read Ingrid's first journal, which was first published as a novel called: **My love We Are Going Home.** Six years later this novel was upgraded and published under the title **The Awakening Clan.** Some of you will start your own mind-drawing group. Whichever way, it's my hope that throughout this workbook every participant will awaken their own Language of Light symbols in order to bring more Soul energy into their physical reality.

Introduction

The language of our inner feelings, drawn out on paper, reveals both in colour, line and symbols how our mental energy mirrors our physical experiences. Our analogue drawings are a reflection of our state of mind at that moment. The drawing below shows how the artist is focussed on the feelings grief after losing a loved one. By going into the pain, we have an opportunity to surrender to it, thereby releasing our emotional connection cords with our past. Any emotional mind games we have with our past, renders us useless and depressed, including holding onto 'expectations of our future that is no more than a state of mind'. Those mind games makes us incapable of moving on in life.

We need to become <u>the observer</u> of our perceived negative, as well as our positive experiences that our mind wants to hold on to — if more 'conscious' soul energy is to embody itself through a physical form. By doodling out our feelings on paper, while staying in the Now moment, we move fully conscious into a stillness where our analytical, lower mental 'programmed' mind cannot enter. Where there is no-mind — there is no pain or sorrow, only peace. True consciousness never dies, only in our 'ego' mind it does.

When we express our inner feelings out on paper, we can confront and work with those energy thought-forms. The analogue drawing above is an example of how our mind expresses feelings of grief when all attachment cords to a loved one are unexpectedly severed.

What is Dying?

A ship sails and I stand watching it till it fades on the horizon. Someone at my side says, "She is Gone" Gone where? Gone from my side. That is all. She is just as large as when I saw her. The diminished size and total loss of sight is in me, not in her.

And just at that moment, when someone at your side says, "She is Gone". There are others who are watching her coming. And others take up a glad shout. "Here she comes!"

And that is Dying

The Power of the Spoken Word

All the Languages that are spoken on the planet form vibrational currents that travel through our auric field like a tornado, a storm, a gale force, a breeze, or a harmonious melody. To verbally interpret 'energy' through a string of words is very limiting, but through doodling, the mind seems to move into a lateral thinking mode and pictorial images, shapes and colours come alive.

Our attention is directed into our akashic records. If the analogue- mind-drawing artist has an intent to awaken soul memories from his or her akashic records, this is one way to do so. In order to understand what previously has been hidden, these drawing activities allow one to tap into a data base that belongs to our observer, the real self.

To awaken our individual Language of Light symbols we have to gain access, at a conscious level, to our soul qualities that are filed away in our etheric blueprint database. We need to listen to our physical, emotional, mental and intuitive/creative bodies. In many people this information may have stayed untapped largely through our technological culture and educational system, but they are there, otherwise their world could not be conceived. There would not be an observer!

Through this Art-analogue Symbolism mind-drawing workbook each participant learns, through their own analogue drawings, what their symbolic signature is. These thought-pictures are often electromagnetic etched imprints that were stored away in the akashic records over eons of time. Every thought, emotion or event that entered a soul while in a holographic etheric plane can be translated through their colour, shape, symbols, texture or even sound. This interpretation can, for many, reveal why they manifest and experience their life's circumstances.

Our physical body has portholes or sensory gates (chakras) through which our 'soul', with the help of the observer, can experience and interpret an earthly experience. The more soul aware we are of these <u>sensory gates</u>, the more we consciously can receive and interpret the energies from the colour spectrum that forms our 'reality' and what they stand for. We learn that through the mind-drawing exercises, which reveal our pictorial visions, symbolic sensations, colour & movement, sound, aroma, shape, texture and depth, our soul communicates with the observer.

Everything that we do as humans has at some level a conscious connection not only with the fingers, but an automatic one with the neural network connecting the fingers to our brain. Therefore every art work can be shaped into a geometric, numeric or symbolic language that translates universal qualities.

This symbolic language we call the Universal Language of Light.

The Power behind the Language of Light.

Often I asked; why don't we remember our soul's wisdom? Why are we so cut off from our inner power, this ability to perceive multidimensional worlds? Why have I created a reality that is not to my liking? On and on it went. Annelies was there for me when I came to my lowest point. I was praying for a release from this life, only to learn that I created my destiny. Only 'I' could make me happy. So where did that lead me? I wanted some tools to work with. There were plenty people out there who all had good advice, but no one could trigger a passion for a specific direction. POWAH must have been waiting for the right moment to come through in the only way that would be meaningful for me; through the medium I was already engaged in, Art-analogue mind-drawing. The Language of Light symbols came later. The following information came from POWAH, so I will share the secret behind the Language of Light. The divine light force that can awaken us from this illusionary world.

The vibrations of creation.

—The language of light are vibrational keys that reflect a quality particle of love. These keys can unlock thought-forms that are locked in a frozen stage within your mind field. It's this energy field that manifests your cellular/molecular structure. During your descent into a lower consciousness realm, the original tones of your creation became distorted. The Language of Light energy symbols represent the original tones and vibrations of creation. Their pure tones form a symphony that restores any thought-form that is not of the light.

Everything on earth had its birth in the factory of the mind, either in God's mind or in man's mind, but no mortal being can think an original thought, he can only borrow God's thoughts and become an instrument to materialize them. Most of your daily thoughts are just bouncing around between these particles (qualities) of love. They are there for every mortal being to embrace, but man is ignorant of his soul's unity consciousness language, and so does not communicate through these symbolic expressions. Because the Language of Light operates on a resonance basis, your thoughts must be of a higher frequency or octave in order to activate these geometric forms into action. This will in turn awaken you to a higher consciousness.

With each incarnation the soul chooses how many Language of Light tones are dispersed during a lifetime. In the past most souls embodied less than 10% of these unity consciousness vibes during a physical lifetime, but in order to manifest a physical ascension, at least 50% of these quality thought forms of love have to be activated.—

Love POWAH

The Law of Electromagnetism

This for me is still the most difficult law to grasp. What is the law of Electromagnetism? In every human being there is a wisdom that knows of a middle pathway. Our mind, versus conscious perception must first sense this pathway between two opposite polarities.

They are Electric (Yang) and Magnetic (Yin) energies.

There is a positive and a negative good, just as there is a positive and a negative evil.

Annelies talks about people who are more electric and others who are more magnetic. Through her ascension-workshop she also mentions people who have radio-active vibes.

- There are people who find nothing wrong with murdering some helpless victim for personal pleasure or profit ...But when I look at nature, a cat sees nothing wrong with killing a mouse...

POWAH explained that we have to recognise the Law of Polarities. Only then are we empowered by our free will to choose. POWAH further explained that when the soul is only embodying less than 10% of its wisdom, then the ego, which is a fragmented inorganic particle of the soul, only perceives the world to either be Black or White, Good or Evil, Hot or cold.....So it is of no use to make any 'judgement' about people who are obviously lacking soul energy. Looking at our world today, how can we motivate them to embody more soul energy? Could there be a reason why some souls seem soulless?

POWAH reminded me that this dilemma has to do with the fall of man's awareness in consciousness. He pointed out that in this dream world we call reality, we perceive everything by our awareness of contrast. All our senses work that way. Our vision sees the differences between light and darkness. Our hearing reacts to the difference between sounds and silence. Our touch responds to distinction between variations of contact-pressures or absence of them. Even our inner senses follow the same laws. We created a world of polarities. Right, left and centre; good, bad and indifferent; positive, negative and neutral. Also, in order to make anything manifest on earth, we have to process it through a whole collection of figures, symbols or words before it appears in material form.

My question was, how do we learn to activate our instinctual nature in order to know what is for the good of all, and what is not?

Trevor, who is an Egyptologist said; "when human literacy married human numeracy our human civilization truly began."

With Trevor's help, because at times POWAH was far too puzzling for me, Trevor told me that all the ancient scripts and symbols were used to tell lies as well as truths. Trevor believed that the co-creator gods allowed this in order to exploit as well as to educate, or to make minds lazy as well as to stretch them. When I wondered why that would be of any benefit to anyone, the following words from POWAH reminded me of people today.

—Thoth, the father of letters offered his pupils the appearance of wisdom, for they read many things without instruction and they therefore seem to know many things, when they were for the most part ignorant.—

The Law of the Gift of our Free Will.

It was Annelies who said that all the books on transformation do not change people, only through practising the ideas that are shared does the body partake through the five senses and stores the experience. In order to change our perception as to how to use the gift of 'free will' in order to be co-creators, we need more psychic power. We know that every thought we have is an energy force. If we want to give it power, we add a feeling to it. It's in the quality of the feeling behind a thought that determines a manifestation. Our feelings can range from fear, hate, anger, hurt, grief, sadness, disappointments to gladness, humourous, happiness, compassion, love, honour and unconditional love for all our creations.

Our 'reality' is created moment by moment. When we engage our five senses, our mental projections, or through the spoken or written word, or by using our imagery visions through creative drawing etc, it's our perceptions of them that creates our reality. Our thought-forms that have the ability to create, are stored in our auric field, which Annelies calls the body of our soul; meaning that our soul consciously projects an 'elemental grid field' that includes all our disunity thought-forms plus the thought-forms that are genetically inherited beliefs and programs from our forefathers. Because of that conditioning, we are compelled to assume that the world of daily life is the one and only world.

It took me a while before I could grasp her concept, but it helped me to rationalize something that at the same time can't be rationalized.

The elemental grid that manifests our physical body

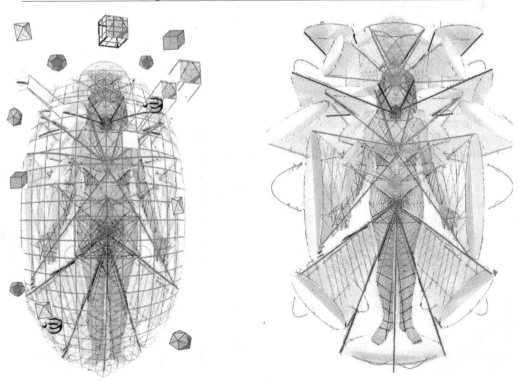

The Law of Space - Time

We all live in the time of the return to the One Language. We call it the 'Language of Light', some call it the 'Language of the Birds', or the 'Mother Tongue'. In the Awakening novels this communication is experienced as Telepathy. There are so many words that may mean the same thing, but our real communication method with each other is nevertheless greatly influenced by the laws of our 'space-time' that combine space and time into a single construct called the **space-time continuum** which Annelies explains in Ingrid's journal **The Awakening Clan**

Could it be possible that we all have forgotten the window into the cycles of time? Most of us no longer grasp the secret behind 'Time'. The ones who upheld the secret of Time may well have been those who believed in outliving the prophecy of the end of the world. There are so many controversial articles on this topic, but in this workbook it is my intent to awaken what some call 'the God gene' through our symbolic expressions.

Time-line, or Time-space of crop formations

First 3D vortex design near Avebury, Wiltshire -30 June 2006

Christian related text mentions our time to be the end of days, or Christians quote from the book of Revelations in the bible.

We feel that the crop formations display knowledge of the times we now live in; that they are symbols that represents a Time-line, or Time-space including celestial alignments.

These patterns also form the basic shapes of our symbolic expressions. When it comes to astronomy and geometry the crop circle makers are second to none.

Are the creators of these formations aliens, or fellow spiritual beings from a higher dimension? I can't truly answer this, but what I have started to become aware of is that we 'humans' are a product, or a creation with one purpose; to evolve.

In ancient times the crop circle makers used 'Mesoamerica' times, a sacred almanac of 260 days in order to communicate to civilizations such as: Olmecs, Teotihuacan-Toltecs, Mayans, Incas, Aztecs and Anasazito. Did our ancestors know then who the crop circle makers were? Were they the creators of the Mayan Calendar?

The Mayan Calendar

Most people are familiar with the Mayan calendar's prophecy that ends in 2012. I've been told that the crop circle symbols that appear each year near Glastonbury, England in our times do so in order to help us to awaken our Codes of Light before we enter the 2012 date. Why?

Introduction 21

Some authors claim that these crop symbols can also be used to decode future events, or can determine the ritual star science that was known in our past going back as far as 3113 BC.

A 3D vortex design perched on the hill near Wiltshire - 20 July 2006

Are they created by Extraterrestrial intelligence?

Most of us agree that there must be an extraterrestrial intelligence that indicates the superior understanding of Earth's (Gaia's) GRID MATRIX with The GRID POINT VALUES!

Annelies' decoding workbook uses a similar grid structure to decode our original blueprint.

Meaningful patterns.

Major World events that are believed to be 100% connected to a 'CONTACT' experience are also a verification of a process where all time-space data is in fact a feed-back to the event in question. In the novels this idea is explained more fully, but in this first workbook we keep our ideas as simple as possible while still tapping into our own Memory configuration (shared- versus distributed-memory) of our brain. Each L or R brain hemisphere uses a local memory storing system and this information is exchanged as messages that

The universal Language of Light symbols in this workbook define the fourth dimension that can be used to establish a time science logbook These universal symbols with their number connections should also be considered as a Galactic Synchronization Model of time in the Universe.

Anyone using the 13 tones of creation symbols together with their individual Language of Light symbols is communicating in advanced symbolic language that can be compared to a mathematical language. These codes form a Matrix.

In Annelies' next decoding workbook 'The Body Codes of Light ' she merges the Language of Light symbol interpretations with the 13 tones of creation.

The God Gene

If this Gene is a reality, since its action has been confirmed in scans of brain activity, our correlation between this gene and reactionary behaviour is indisputable. This doesn't mean that there's one gene that makes people believe in God, but it refers to the fact that humans inherit a predisposition to be spiritual – to reach out and look for a higher being.

We live in a Genetic world, fast sometimes frightening – and potentially very lucrative. We as human beings must strive to evolve in order to become co-creators on a Galactic level of awareness. A principle of 'Evolution' is Immortality, it can't be anything else.

The Five Processes of our four lower bodies through which we Manifest our Reality

I have Annelies' permission to use her descriptions of the five awareness levels throughout this workbook. I want to refrain from using a terminology that describes the supernatural because the real essential of greatness in the human spirit is not written in books, nor can this be found in the world we call reality. It is written into the inner consciousness of everyone who intensely searches for perfection in creative achievements.

On the <u>first level of our awareness</u> of this physical world most people still hold onto this reality as being the only world they know. Only when life gets difficult or events on a global scale start to erupt in chaos and violence, many people start to question the reason for their existence. What then tends to happen is that many people start to have a desire to become aware.

Ingrid is a truly good example of that awareness level. She described through her journal what happened to her 'reality' when she activated a mental telepathy with her soul.

The five stages of creativity that are described throughout the course, are often mentioned so that you the participant can reflect on which level you are manifesting your 'life'. It's this level which has created your world of 'reality'.

How this process ties in with our four lower bodies will be addressed in Annelies' decoding workbook: The Body Codes of Light.

Each creative stage reflects each level of awareness when you take on the role as your observer. Again and again I discovered that the way to universal truth lies in the the way we perceive it.

My experience throughout the mind-drawing exercises is that when we trust in the inner universal power, it automatically draws forth the trust of the people one deals with. We start to change our reality like Ingrid did.

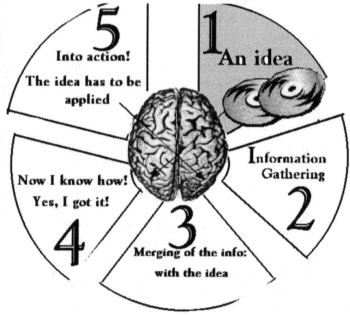

Namasté

Tieneke de Beer

The Five Stages of Creativity

During the years that I gave drawing skill classes, I used the following 5 creative steps to help the students enhance their perception skills. Everything we create seems to follow a similar formula.

Whether we bake a cake, build a house, plan a holiday or create any art form, the five steps are the same.

<u>First stage</u>. We have to have an <u>idea</u>! We need to know what we want to manifest in our lives in order to move on to the next stage. If it is a loving relationship like Ingrid and Toon have, we need to know what we want in a partner and what qualities we have ourselves that would attract such a partner. Then the <u>idea</u> has to be investigated.

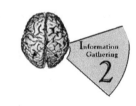

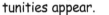

We move into the <u>Second stage</u> in order to <u>gather information</u> surrounding our idea. There is no time frame as to how long we stay in each stage, but when we use this formula, as we journey through the chakras in this workbook, we become aware at which stage most of our obstacles or opportunities appear.

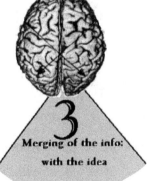

After we feel we have gathered enough information we move to the <u>Third stage</u>.

Now we try the idea out with the backing of the gathered information. This is the third stage where miscalculations are corrected. This is the rehearsal stage. This is the stage where we have to release old patterns in order to replace them with new ideas that belong to the new paradigm, or a new dream. Most of us still roam around on this level of awareness.

We are the observer of our own creation, our own dream, our own manifestations. We would not experience 'life' the way we do if we were not at the same time our own observer. The 22 cards help us to observe the vibrations of our mental, physical and emotional energies. It also reveals the quality and its characteristics of our soul energy.

After this third rehearsal stage we move into the <u>Fourth stage</u> where the energy of synchronicity guides us to improve our preparation in order to manifest our desires. We find solutions in order to overcome obstacles. Brainstorming sessions are fruitful. We are our own observer.

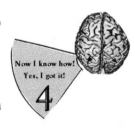

24 The Language of Light

This stage can also be addictive; meaning, many people never move from this stage into the fifth stage where all the first four stages have to be applied! We all know people who say: " I always wanted to ... travel..or write a book!"

The <u>fifth stage</u> means that now you have to apply action!
Now your idea has to manifest itself. If it has not, you have to look at which stage your idea has procrastinated.

When we take this 5 stage formula and apply it to our awakening process, we will soon recognize which sensory gate (chakra) needs our attention in order to make a shift in consciousness.

Each Chakra vortex is related to our 5 physical senses of smell, hearing, seeing, touching and tasting. It's our intuitive sense that needs to be reinstated in order to experience the mental telepathy that Ingrid and Toon reveal in Ingrid's journal:

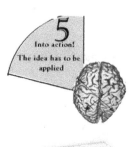

The Awakening Clan.

Let's look again at an overview of the 5 stages & 5 levels

The desire to become aware, creates a motivation

- This <u>First stage</u>, or level of awareness can be interpreted as our first seven years in this life time.
- Or the moment where our awakening has started.
- Or a new (1-7 year) relationship. In this workbook we use it as the stage where ideas are born.
- This is the stage where the Root Chakra acts as our guide.
- This chakra is the sensory gate where our preprogrammed beliefs, survival and instinctual patterns are stored.

- Or, if we talk of a <u>Young Soul Age.</u> Meaning that only between 5 to 10 % of our soul energy is embodied.
- On this level our emotional levels are often reacting from a very superstitious perception and we frighten very easily. There is very little consequential thought.
- We are childlike, live in the moment but are ignorant or even aggressive.

Other teachings say that only two strands of DNA are activated. We are often very connected to nature, love rituals and feel safe with our family's religious beliefs. We still hold a belief that others are to blame for our misfortunes.

The Five Stages of Creativity 25

In Ingrid's journal Annelies describes that the rules of her ascension board game revolve around an energy scrub. Man's subconscious mind must be cleared of all his diligently stored past experiences. They form our beliefs, past vows, karmic memories and pains (many of which are lodged blockages in our energy fields and bodies) That means that most of us have many Base Chakra issues to release, especially to do with obstacles that are survival driven. These energy blocks have created obstacles in the journey back to where we came from.

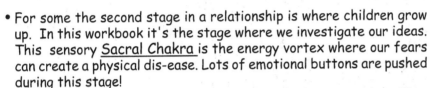

To become aware that we are unaware creates an awareness.

- This <u>Second stage</u> often reflects our education years. They are (7-14-21-28 years) or our soul searching years.

- For some the second stage in a relationship is where children grow up. In this workbook it's the stage where we investigate our ideas. This sensory <u>Sacral Chakra</u> is the energy vortex where our fears can create a physical dis-ease. Lots of emotional buttons are pushed during this stage!

- At this stage we talk of a <u>Questioning Soul Age.</u> Meaning that 10 to 12 % of our soul's energy is now embodied. On this level we still need rules to live by and rely on higher authority to tell us what to do. Most of us on this awareness level still need lots of approval and still see things only as black and white. We do not like change! Image is important to us and we often will pursue traditional careers that promote our standing in the community. We make good citizens and are conscientious. We will do the right thing and love to create rules in order to create structure in society. On this level of awareness we also can be rigid and dogmatic.

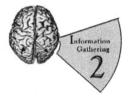

—In Ingrid's journal Annelies states that at all times mankind must become aware of his/her own thoughts words and actions in every moment.—

This means a release of all negative emotions, negative thought forms, and negative ego actions. This integration process belongs to the Cosmic and Eternal order to which we all belong but we need to understand the Universal Principles to be aware.

Each level seems to respond to a different 'time frame'. When we move into the <u>Third stage</u> of awareness we become like trapeze artists that live on the edge of two realities.

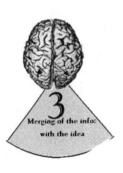

Letting go of the old. This means detachment.

26 The Language of Light

When I asked Annelies if she believed that a soul could be evil, her reply was; " The Eastern belief is that evil exists on the lowest planes of existence, therefore it is best to advance oneself spiritually beyond these as rapidly as evolution allows, so arriving at a state of heaven and beyond it to that nirvana where; 'The wicked cease from troubling and the weary are at rest'. The Western attitude, on the other hand, is to come to grips with evil on its own ground and defeat it by every possible means."

This reminded me of our Left and Right modes of thinking. Both awareness levels of the northern hemisphere and the southern hemisphere accept the presence of evil, but deals with it completely differently.

Before I carry on I would like to add a story, which I'm not sure is true, but the source from where I read it from is certainly the work of a master.

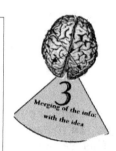

A Salvation Army captain once said: "I suppose you think that we all want to go to heaven when we die? Well we don't. The ambition of every true Salvationist, is to get into Hell." When asked by her startled audience why this should be so, she continued, "If only enough of us could get into Hell we'd soon put a stop to all that suffering. We'd convert the Devil, clean the place up, and make sure the people in it were penitent enough to enter Heaven. The Devil daren't let us in there for fear of what we'd do. There's endless numbers of us hammering away on his doors and he's too scared to let us in. He's a coward."

- <u>This Third stage</u> is often reached (on a mundane level) during our career years, work years or when our direction of interest is awakened. (28-35-42 years)
- For some their soul purpose has become known. It's in the third stage in a relationship where children leave the home and where we explore and try out our original idea or dreams.
- This is the energy gateway of our <u>Solar Plexus</u> Lots of changes happen when this chakra has completely opened!
- This energy vortex, when active, will stir our emotional as well as our mental body into action.
- This stage is the most trying level for our soul to be motivated to embody more of itself. On this level we learn to let go of the old through means of detachment.
- On this level we talk of a <u>Mature Soul Age.</u> Meaning that between 12 to 18 % of our soul energy is embodied. Today the world is mostly driven by people who are power driven. Independence and competitiveness are very strong

ego-driven emotions but they prepare us to release issues that do not work anymore.
- Some of us stay at this mundane level and do not believe in an Higher Power. When we are dead, it is all over. Some of us are so power driven, we do not take into account the consequences of our decisions. We don't have much insight into our own or other people's behaviours. Many of our leaders are very industrious, create new and efficient structures and accumulate great wealth, but they can also be pushy and self-righteous. On this level an almost divided awareness level is merging.

- People who are spiritually driven prepare their physical, emotional and mental bodies in order to replace them with wide-ranging insights and a deep intuitive understanding about physical life.
- Complete self-acceptance (This means integration) For many people this third stage awakens their Heart Chakra. Then they move into the fourth stage.

- For many this happens during their retirement years. For some their soul purpose has become a daily meditation.(49-56-63-70 years) In relationships, or when people are on their own, this is where grandchildren play an important role.
- It is also the preparation stage for when people move into the the illumination stage surrounding soul purpose ideas, or you synchronize with people of like mind or you have many 'Aha' moments.
- On this level we talk of a Mature compassionate Soul Age. We do not need others to agree with-or approve of us. All creative expressive endeavours appeal to us. We recognise that we live in our own dream.

—In Ingrid's journal Annelies describes this level as the incubation stage. The Time is at Hand! On this level we become servers of the light upon planet earth and lay the foundations for the next quantum leap in our Spiritual evolution.

By diligently clearing and releasing the causes of limitations in the past and their effects in our present, we release that which no longer serves us, in order to make room for communication from the Higher Intelligence and the forthcoming higher intensity vibrations.

- As more of our soul energy is embodying our physical form, our lives seem like an emotional roller-coaster ride. We choose to live in homes that reflect our individuality. Many of us have by now embodied 20 to 30% of our soul energy. This still means that our personalities (with the help of inorganic beings) are still 70 to 80 % in control, but we are moving into the fourth stage where our Throat chakra is activated and we will learn to speak our truth with compassion.

—In Ingrid's journal Annelies calls this level the tail end of the third stage. Complete self acceptance has to be reached emotionally. Our Heart chakras are opened and we integrate with the Higher Self, our observer and our Inner Guide by completely enabling the physical, emotional and mental bodies of the lower self to become totally aligned and integrated. We awaken the dreamer within.

28 The Language of Light

Integration - this is usually an illumination stage in our lives.

- The <u>Fourth stage</u> is the <u>Throat and the Third Eye Chakra gateway;</u> the cosmic vortex where our inner truth must be expressed. The earlier one gets to open this awareness level in life the better!
- Only a few people reach this level of awareness. From an independent individual you became an interdependent citizen where service to humanity is priority number one. If the ascension path is chosen, lots of universal guidance will enrich and bring joy into one's life. Many people on this level still battle with poor self-esteem issues.
- At this stage we want to move away from a social life and surround ourselves with nature or connect to all in love.

—In Ingrid's journal Annelies calls it the Illumination stage. Going with the current flow! This stage will greatly accelerate our Soul's progress to travel in an awakened consciousness through the physical vehicle. Then ultimate transfiguration of our physical form into the vibrations of our light bodies, which belong to the higher dimensions, will be the next evolutionary journey of the I AM Presence.

- Most people who reach this stage of awareness have worked on themselves starting from the ages of 14-35-49-56 years. Relationships are only formed or stay together if both parties have a soul mission they can share. Now the original idea has to be applied!
- Many call this the Old Soul Age but that could be misinterpreted. Many children who are born today bring in a lot more Soul energy from the start of their lives. We live in special times where many souls, who have awakened a great deal in their last incarnation can make this their last incarnation. Some souls have only had two or three lives on this planet, but they are still very advanced souls.
- For many on this level with the help of the Language of Light more soul qualities can be embodied in order to cope with the physical changes.
- On this level we are completely spiritually driven. 40 to 50% of soul energy is integrated on this level.
- At this stage we want to move away from a mundane social life and surround ourselves with all beings on earth that like you, have a love for all.

- Many of us go through many changes. Emotionally we have to detach from people who are not on a soul driven spiritual path. This creates great turmoil. All we want is an inner joy, and what we often experience during this stage is the loss of material, mental and emotional things like a secure job, our possessions or the people who are not on a spiritual path. It's on this level that we have to let go. We have to totally be in the now. We have to completely be in trust.

—In Ingrid's journal Annelies calls the fifth stage a Verification stage. At this stage the integration of the three polarities of our subconscious and conscious mind with our Super-Conscious or Divine mind will occur. In our scriptures some of the people who reached this level appeared as Jesus Christ, Krishna, Buddha, Lau Tsu and, who knows, even Ra. At no time must we pledge our devotion to any of these deities. We must travel this ascension path on our own without any attachment to gurus, masters or enlightened beings. Even the 'messenger must in the end be released in order to physically ascend.

Freedom - Expressing the power on one.

- This <u>fifth level</u> Annelies also calls Freedom through Unity consciousness (Applied through Action)
- Only a few people reach this level of awareness. These people are able to transcend the personality. They have a rich inner life and can transcend the illusion that comprises the physical plane.
- This level was rarely reached in the past but we live in times when many that have chosen the ascension path shall receive lots of universal guidance. This is the stage of the Crown chakra that has opened and connected to the higher spiritual chakras.
- This is the soul-field-file from where the Language of Light will come streaming into the physical realm through the 6 lower chakras in order to speed up the vibratory rate of the physical/molecular structure for the ascension process to start.
- Many will receive "Messages" from an inner source. They usually come by means of "implantations" of coded consciousness which might be termed spiritual shorthand, or cosmic computerese.
- On this level the person that has received these communications from a higher consciousness is then responsible for translating this into extended terms of whatever earthly language might be required.
- On this level of awareness there are worlds within worlds, dreams within the dream. We start to create portholes into different realities during our dream time.

An Art-analogue introduction

How do I express my thoughts on paper?

How do I draw out any thoughts in colour, shape or texture without drawing any picture or pictorial vision?

How do I draw any thought on paper that has no words or symbol that could in any way symbolically be interpreted?

Those are the questions that most people have when they start with mind-drawing. All I tell them is to become like a child. Just Play.

- Allow yourself to become totally free and spontaneous on paper.
- Treat the paper like the child does.
- Allow your thoughts to travel through your arm into your hand and out through the pencil onto the paper.
- Anything is allowed except try not to make symbols or images at first.
- Get familiar with your own way of thinking.
- Everybody is unique in their expression of who they are and how they perceive their world. So are you.
- With permission from my students I have included some of their Art-analogue expressions.
- See if you can connect with the energy their art-analogue drawings reflect to you.
- Don't copy any of them. Allow your creative /intuitive body to fully partake and leave your persona out of your creative drawing meditations.

Nadine - Tieneke

During May 1995 these mind-drawings were my first glimpses of people's energy fields in certain moods.

An Art-analogue introduction 31

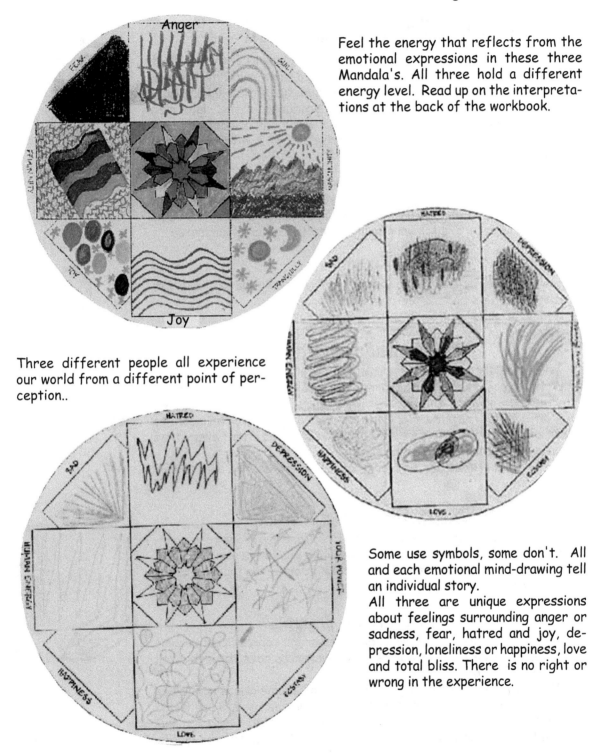

Feel the energy that reflects from the emotional expressions in these three Mandala's. All three hold a different energy level. Read up on the interpretations at the back of the workbook.

Three different people all experience our world from a different point of perception..

Some use symbols, some don't. All and each emotional mind-drawing tell an individual story.

All three are unique expressions about feelings surrounding anger or sadness, fear, hatred and joy, depression, loneliness or happiness, love and total bliss. There is no right or wrong in the experience.

The Tools you Need

If you are on your own, you need to be in a quiet place where you will not be disturbed during the duration of your mind-drawings. If you are on your own or in a group, play some meditative music in the background.

All the formats of the exercises are produced in the right size throughout this workbook. You can use this workbook as your personal symbolic diary, or photo copy each exercise. Treat it with honour the way you would treat a loved one!

Go through the workbook first and take a look at the formats of your Language of Light cards. The idea is that you cut your Language of Light cards out and paste them on an A4 sheet so you can take them to be colour copied. One card is for your booklet and the other is laminated.

Tools

- Pencils, colour pencils, felt pens or any other media you best express yourself in this book, or on photo-copy paper.
- A hand or stand mirror.

Your Mental preparation:

- Ask your higher self to partake in the following exercises.
- Write on page 34, or on a separate piece of paper, what you want to achieve throughout this mind-drawing course.
- Always state an intent before you proceed. If you have the intent to ascend during this life time, make this a conscious intent every time before you start these exercises.
- Invite your soul to embody more of its divine energy during your drawing.

Your Emotional preparation:

- Give yourself a hug before you start. If you are in a group form a circle and hold hands for a few minutes while you invite your persona, with all it's characteristics, to partake in order to transform for the good of all.

Create a dream journal

- Dreaming is a process of awakening, of gaining control. Our dreams are portholes into other worlds. Our awareness goes through a veil or tunnel into other realms.
- We need to have lots of psychic energy to become aware not to get mixed with inorganic beings that add foreign energy into our field.
- For some this might be a strange way to look at it but I have a suspicion that science fiction writers are not all that far off the mark!

The First Stage

Ideas from your Rational mind

- Your welcome page
* Your rational mind. (Any creation starts with and idea.)
* The Seven Psychic centres versus your physical senses.
  - Imagery through a Keyhole
  - The gift of Compassion and Empathy
  - The gift of Telepathy.
  - The gift of Clairvoyance and Prophecy
* Discover your strength through doodling.
  - 12 directions your perception realities move to.
* The Base Chakra (your security centre)
  - The colours and symbols about security issues
  - The colours and symbols about fear issues
  - The colours and symbols about inventiveness
* Your first Language of Light Symbol
* Your first insight.

Welcome to your Art-analogue-symbolism workshop

- **1.** Please write in the first box what you would like to experience from this mind drawing workshop. As you write, invite the presence of your higher self energy to take part. (This is later studied as part of an exercise)
- **2.** On the envelope on the next page write your postal address the same way as if you would send it to yourself. (This is later studied as part of an exercise)
- **3.** Write your e-mail address (if any).and phone number within the arrow format under your first box. (This will later be used as part of an exercise.)

Welcome Page 35

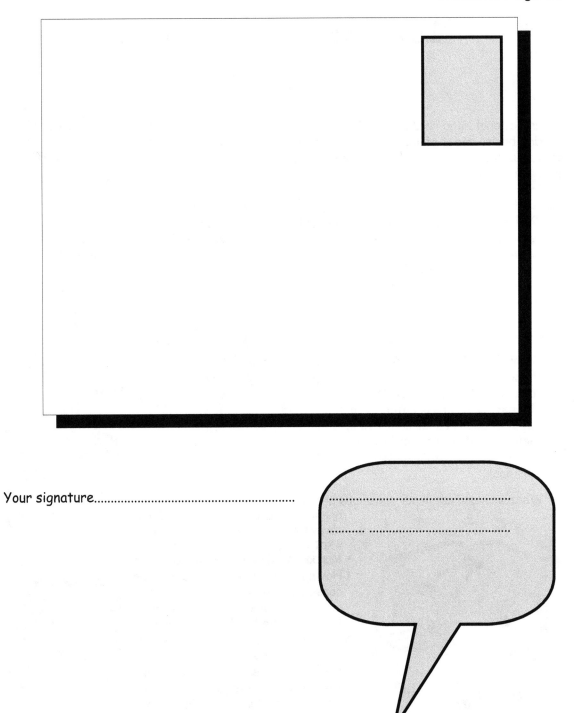

Your signature..

36   The Language of Light

Level one: Your Rational Mind
Where ideas are born.

Our Rational Mind versus our conscious awareness mind on a day to day basis. Most of our daily thoughts stream through this first conscious awareness level. Throughout this workbook we associate this awareness level with both our Base and Throat chakra.

From our energy vortex, the **Base Chakra**, most of our thoughts that deal with survival issues, taken from our past or future, stream through this Red Ray frequency. When we say Red, this does not mean a solid colour red, the colours orange and yellow are also seen in this vortex. The longest wavelength in our visible spectrum is Red. This energy is an outgoing vibration mostly related to aggressiveness and conquest. POWAH says that many inorganic beings are addicted to this energy.

We call this our <u>Security Centre</u>

- Throughout this workbook we work on two levels. Our <u>mundane</u> day to day reality level, and our <u>soul level</u>.
- The exercises are created in such a way that each reader can read up on their mind-drawings on <u>both levels</u> at the interpretation section of this workbook.

- What we manifest in our conscious physical lives is a mirror to our inner life. This universal truth is not always easy to swallow but that is what being human is all about.
- Mundane level means our physical level!
- Having an inner power to become a conscious co-creator now is the most rewarding state to be in on this mundane level of awareness.
- The illustrations on the right reflect that even during just any day in our lives we can recognise the 5 creative stages.
- Any project, plan, invention, or even a relationship seems to travel through the same five stages.

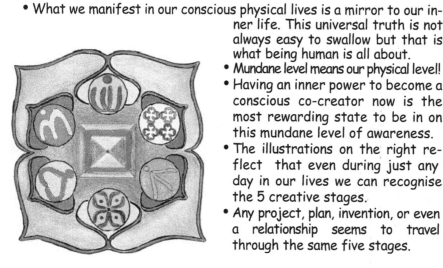

Level One / Stage one 37

The Seven Psychic Centres
Through the 5 creative stages

Ideas from our soul level

Many of the mind-drawing exercises are transmitted through our seven conscious awareness levels.

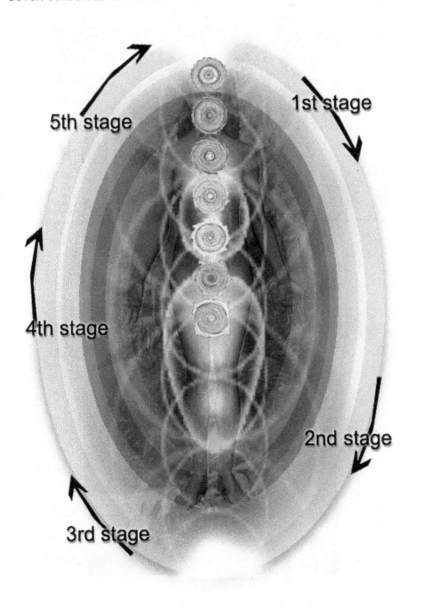

1st stage
2nd stage
3rd stage
4th stage
5th stage

Any Creation starts with an Idea

First exercise on a mundane level

- When you start with your mind-drawing journey, take any idea you might have that has become a desire that you want to manifest in your life. **You have to start with an idea.**
- Even when you want to bake a cake, you have to know what you are going to bake!
- Take an idea that could take around 8 weeks to materialise.
- Every human being has the ability to manifest anything they want out of life......providing it is for the good of all.
- Believe me that is very important. Most of the time we attract the very thing we least wanted. Why? Our thoughts are overshadowed by our egos, so our unconscious divine mind, who cannot discern between good or bad, light or dark, cold or hot,.......attracts, on an energy level, what is in our thoughts!

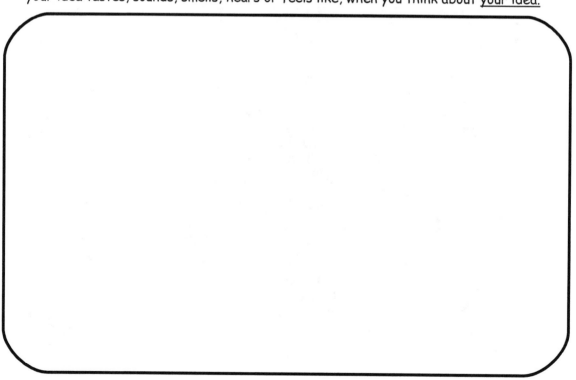

- Draw with colour pencils, in an Art-analogue way, in the box below what your idea tastes, sounds, smells, hears or feels like, when you think about <u>your idea.</u>

Imagery through a keyhole
First exercise on a soul level

It is very important to state an intent. Our soul knows why it has chosen this incarnation and it is fully aware what lessons or distorted programming has to be transformed into the light. Your Soul passion is closely linked to the ideas that you have on a mundane level. This first art-analogue mind-drawing will stimulate and awaken what was hidden before.

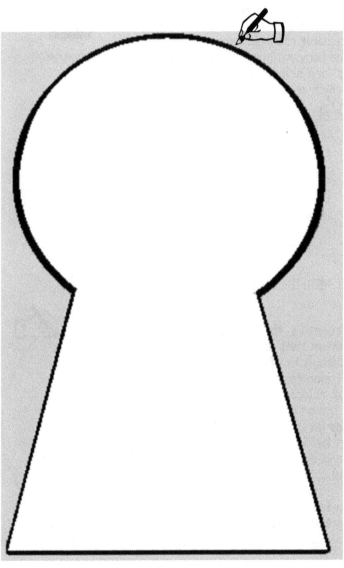

- Always start by inviting your higher self, the real you, what feels right for you to partake in all the drawing exercises.
- Have some nice music playing softly in the background.
- Read the instructions first and then 'mentally' follow them, while you stay attuned as to how your body feels 'physically'.
- Be aware of your five senses, when you recall what thoughts you have unconsciously recorded at the time of your last meal?

*Close your eyes and leave the outer world..
*Enter into your inner world, the world of ideas................................
*Allow your thoughts and feelings to turn into colour and shaping images..

- What are your emotional <u>feelings</u> around your last meal?
- If your feelings could make <u>sounds</u>, what would they sound like?
- Is there a <u>scent</u> associated with your <u>feelings</u>?
- If your feelings have <u>colour</u>, what are they?
- Do your feelings have a <u>texture</u> or a pattern?
- What kind of <u>rhythm</u> would they have?

Now start drawing

We are all Psychics!

Second exercise on a mundane level

Your Psychic Feeling centres are:

The first <u>Base Chakra</u>, the third <u>Solar Plexus</u> and the fourth <u>Heart Chakra</u>.

- Some people think with "physical" sensations. It's the activity of both the Base, Solar Plexus and Heart chakra. It's through the Heart centre (when opened) that we attract the gift of Compassion and Empathy.
- This **Psychic Feeling** is the most accessible of all our reception areas.
- When we are reacting from our emotional body, we "<u>think</u>" from this centre.
- Also our "gut feelings" or "instincts" are helpful in order to identify which auric colour resonates with "feelings". (This psychic centre is very active in people who are Practising Feng-Shui or colour therapy) This is both a Left Hemisphere and a Right Hemisphere thinking-mode function.

See interpretation section

Draw out which numbers or/and colours come into your mind?

<u>Our Psychic Feelings are connected with the sense of sight and smell.</u>

- This Feeling Psychic vortex is receptive to any emotionally charged thoughts. I mean that any past memory that is still potent enough to affect your behaviour now, you will manifest. Those reactive feelings need to be released in order to open the Heart chakra, the bridge into the higher conscious awareness levels.
- As you close your eyes, feel the first two lower vortexes spinning wider and wider and draw in the circle the colours and shapes that appeal to you at this moment.
- When you have finished, write in a feeling word that comes to mind while you were drawing.

....

We are all Psychics!

Second exercise on a soul level

Through the following four Soul level exercises we are establishing through which psychic centres our soul is most likely to release the qualities of the Language of light. These qualities will help us to bring back any dysfunctional energies that are locked within our auric field, into balance.

Your Psychic Feeling Centre Channel

Before you do the following mind-drawing exercise, stand up (if you are unable to, do it on a chair) and follow the physical movements of the Salute to the Sun on your right.

- What you feel can be as mild as 'butterflies' or as strong as a knot in the pit of your stomach. Our Solar Plexus is like a master antenna where the autonomic nervous system provides direct access and is linked to every major organ and most endocrine glands.
- In order to activate our psychic feeling centre we are going to communicate to the <u>body avatar</u>.
- Through our following mind-drawing exercise allow the <u>body avatar</u> to speak to you as you let the colours, shapes and patterns travel through your arm into your hand on this paper......
- Let your soul speak to you as you draw in an art-analogue way your thoughts that come up as you focus on your solar plexus.

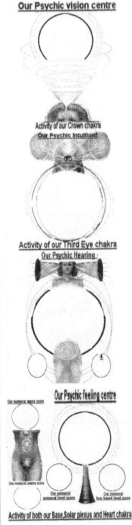

We are all Psychics!

Third exercise on a mundane level

Throughout Ingrid's journal: 'The Awakening Clan the gift of mental telepathy is explored in her story. The depth of intimacy that she experienced with Toon and her friends is something most of us would only dream of. Many people are not even aware that they are telepathic. They think that the words they hear are just their own inner dialogue with themselves. I daresay for many that is just what it is, so express through your drawings the words you mentally hear, and what their colours are.

Our Psychic Hearing centres are:

The Second Sacral Chakra and Fifth Throat Chakra.

Draw out which numbers or/and colours come into your mind?

- Some people literally 'hear' their thoughts. Telepathy often starts with the voice that speaks from within, but it takes a lot more inner focus to hear others speak mentally.
- Mental telepathy will only happen after the Heart chakra is fully activated, because without genuine compassion you can't connect with others in this way.
- By listening to your body's needs, by establishing a connection with your 'body avatar', you will greatly activate your psychic sensitivity.
- When we only use our Left-brain 'linear' mode of thinking, this inner mental dialogue can make some of us very analytical. Academically trained people have to overcome this obstacle, before they activate their psychic hearing centre. This psychic gift is very helpful for analysing symbolic expressions in art. **Psychic Hearing** also helps to assimilate if our giving and receiving is in balance.
- This psychic hearing is connected to the sense of hearing and taste.
- Feel the Sacral and the Throat vortex spinning wider and wider and draw in the colour energy that you hear or sense as it enters into your ears.
- When you are finished, write in a feeling word that comes to mind...

Level One / Stage one 43

We are all Psychics!

Third exercise on a soul level

If you already know what your soul passion is, then this psychic centre would already be active. If you don't know as yet what activity, topic of interest or creativity gives you the most joy then learn to listen to your inner voice. Invite your soul to partake and make the intent to live this live through your soul passion.

Our Psychic Hearing Centre Channel.

- How sensitive are you? Can you hear when someone is lying? Are you over activated when you can cut the atmosphere in a room with a knife?
- Shut the world outside and invite your soul energy to enter any of the 7 psychic centre channels.

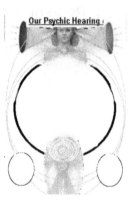

- Draw from your intuitive mind your favourite centre at that moment.

44 The Language of Light

We are all Psychics!

Fourth exercise on a mundane level

This Psychic gift is definitely bestowed on Annelies. She always says that mine can be activated if I let go of my feeling of not being good enough. This gift cannot be awakened if we carry any feelings of low self esteem in whatever form shape or size.

Our Psychic Intuitive/Creative centre

The Sixth Third Eye Chakra and the Seventh Crown Chakra

- Some people think 'intuitively.' It's the gift of Clairvoyance or some people think 'visually.' It's the gift of Prophecy

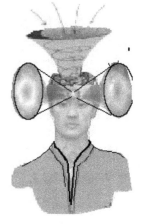

Draw out which numbers or/and colours come into your mind?

- This instantaneous knowing helps us to make a decision when we are contemplating our creative process.
- This awareness is very helpful in observing if an artwork of any description has aesthetic appeal.

- This sixth psychic vortex resonates to beauty and is also a very Right-mode function. It activates our sense of Inner seeing.
- Our sixth sense or Third Eye energy vortex helps us to activate our visual-inner seeing skills.
- Before you do this mind-drawing, light a candle and stare into the flame. Let the music interact with you as you are focussing on the light.
- Now allow your Crown energy vortex to spin round the light and observe where your thoughts are taking you.
- Remember your first idea? Now move onto the second stage and start gathering information surrounding your idea.
- Feel this vortex spinning wider and wider. Access the feelings that are pulsating in a rainbow of colours. Draw them out in an art-analogue way and write down one feeling word.

....

We are all Psychics!

Fourth exercise on a soul level

In this mind-drawing exercise I want you to experience shifting your intuitive/creative body from one perception point to another. This means we are now moving our perception point away from the realm of the rational mind. We are now 'seeing' imageries that our intellectual rational mind cannot interpret. Many people who channel or hear inner voices think that they have shifted their consciousness into a realm where evolved beings can interact with them.

Annelies warned me that many people have lost their power to the voices or visions they encountered. I was very distraught when Annelies said that hearing a voice from a light being did not mean that they were light beings. Sometimes they are inorganic beings that need your energy.

- Inorganic beings are actually energy balls that are fragmented lost personas. They are within every human's energy field. They affect our behaviour if they are in full control. Often we refer to them as our personality or our EGOS.
- When we make an intent to live this life for our soul passion, we have to address these inorganic beings. Through this last Psychic awareness exercise we ask them to move aside and allow our intuitive/ creative body to start seeing the symbols that reflect the Language of our Soul.
- Seeing mental pictures is helpful in drawing, sculpting, painting and especially fantasy art. Many of the old masters were truly experts at this.
- At the beginning of the computer age.our technology has made our intuitive/ creative body sluggish. Television, movies, and the computer technology temporary replaced this psychic skill.
- But since nothing that we create is useless, in the last ten years many people started to use our technology to bring these creative skills back. More than ever before our imagery abilities are stimulated by the art expressions that are created by the technology of today.

- Especially in our western world our towns are decorated with kaleidoscopic moving imageries to communicate a message.
- Bring in the energy that reflects your soul's passion. Allow your mind to travel away from your rational mind and think the unthinkable possibilities and make them come alive!
- Take the feeling word from your mundane exercise and express it again in an art-analogue way.

What do your doodles reveal?
Through the twelve created formats

Through my drawing skill art classes in the past, I discovered that my students' line drawings were often stiff and unimaginative until I asked them to doodle away.
This was done without project based ideas or an agenda. While we were talking about the art of drawing they had to doodle. I created different formats to see if that made any difference to the drawing and found that it did.
On this page some of my students' doodling examples show how each person is unique in their doodling expressions.

- Every waking moment our minds interpret what our physical senses experience.

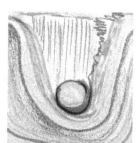

- Throughout this workbook our mind is seen as an energy force that permeates our auric field that Annelies calls the body of our soul.
- Energy as we experience it is worded as a frequency, a sound, light-wave, vibration or a pulsation. If we contemplate this further, we can say that our mind from then on creates projections of colours and shapes within our auric field.

Something hidden?

- It's in our individual symbols, colour and line drawings that we draw out our often hidden thought-forms.
- These thought-forms are our basic building blocks that in turn creates a holographic field we call reality.
- Since our holographic energy field is multidimensional, our auric field has many different layers of vibrations simultaneously projecting a physical, mental, emotional and a creative intuitive projection of our perceptions.

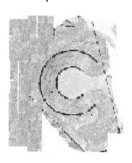

The mind can speak through many forms and shapes.

The colours and shapes our mind sees become symbols to each individual that creates them. If we acknowledge that our soul is a vibrational akashic library that hold all our records, then we know that an untold abundance of information, skills, talents and abilities are still dormant.

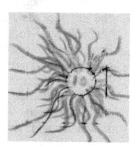

- The following 12 doodling exercises must be done quickly and without any agenda in mind.
- It helps to be in company when you doodle.
- Have a drawing pad with a pencil near your phone and copy any of the 12 formats.
- Each format has been created to stimulate your mind to create line drawings that fit within that format.
- Any type of drawing is allowed like analogue, symbolic or pictorial but rather use a pencil.
- Don't copy, be original!

Self discovery.
Feel the energy.

Many pathways

Level One / Stage one 47

Your twelve life style focussed doodles.

Access your holistic right brain thinking mode

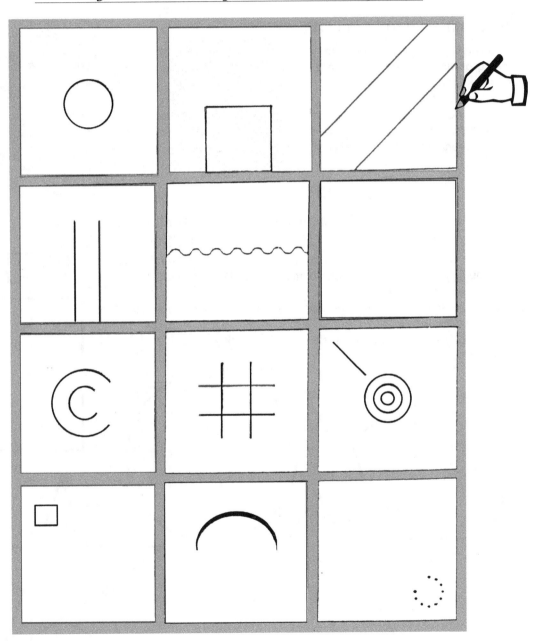

The Psychic Channel where ideas are Born

First exercise on a mundane level

To be motivated to become aware

On the mundane level in this mind-drawing exercise you are working on an idea you have chosen to work with throughout this workbook.

In the first stage the Root (base)chakra is the energy channel, where our preprogrammed beliefs and instinctual behaviour patterns influence our perceptions. This security orientated channel has a great effect on our creative originality exercises.

Guidelines:

What format and which colour might trigger feelings you have about your <u>personal security issues</u>.

- When you think about your idea mentally travel within and explore <u>through your 5 senses</u> which format feels like an obstacle towards your manifestation.
- Observe how each format guides or influences your thoughts as you colour them in.
- Start drawing with no intent to create a work of art, just be in the moment.

Level One / Stage one 49

Any thought that influences your Conscious mind

First exercise on a soul level

Guidelines:

What colour or symbol reflects your anxiety surrounding security issues
- Read the 8 words and translate your feelings by drawing in colour, shape or symbol what colours and analogue expressions come up with each word.
- Rate the number level of your intensity feeling between 1 to 12 (1 Being low, 12 being high) surrounding each of the fear-based attention points.
- Think of one more security based issue that was not included and add it in.

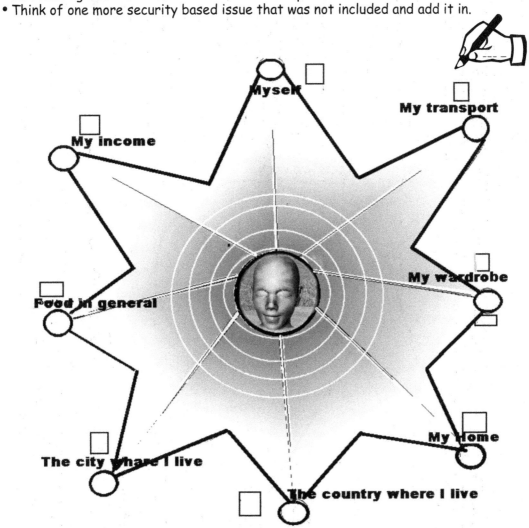

The Psychic Channel where ideas are Born

Second exercise on a mundane level

The energy that represents 'Fear' is slightly different for everyone but no matter what, these fragmented inorganic energy balls will always be an obstacle when we want to manifest something in our lives.

- The following exercises were created in order to acknowledge and release any <u>fear based</u> thought-forms that are trapped into your auric field.

Guidelines:

What format and which colour might trigger feelings you have about your <u>personal fear issues.</u>

- When you think about your idea and what, where or how you feel surrounding your idea, mentally travel within and explore <u>through your 5 senses</u> which format might hold any fear-based energy that might stop you from manifesting your idea, and what colour it has.
- Observe how each format guides your thoughts as you colour them in.
- Start drawing with no intent to create a work of art, just be in the moment.

Level One / Stage one 51

Any thought is <u>stored</u> by your Conscious mind

Second exercise on a soul level

Guidelines:

What colour or symbol reflects the fears you recognise surrounding security issues

- Read the 8 words and translate your feelings by drawing in colour, shape or symbol what colours and analogue expressions come up with each word.
- Rate the number level of your intensity feeling between 1 to 12 (1 Being low, 12 being high) surrounding each of the fear-based attention points.
- Think of one more fear-based issue that was not included and add them in.

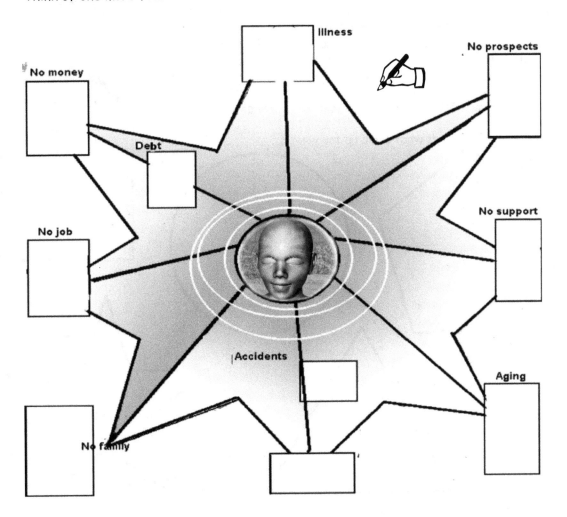

The Psychic Channel where ideas are Born

Third exercise on a mundane level

We all harbour feelings of admiration for the talents in others, but rarely do we see them in ourselves. Each person at birth has brought in talents, qualities and gifts to be explored for the good of all, but many people never discover their uniqueness.
- The following exercises were created in order to awaken or bring to your attention the talents, qualities and gifts you admire the most in others.

Guidelines:

What format and colour might trigger feelings you admire the most in others

- When you think about your idea and what feelings you have surrounding your idea, mentally travel within and explore <u>through your 5 senses</u> which format inspires you the most when you think of your idea, and what colour guided you.
- Observe how each format guides your thoughts as you colour them in.
- Write in a few words what came up for you ....

Level One/ Stage One 53

Any quality that inspires your Conscious mind
Third exercise on a soul level

Guidelines:

1.........NEAT........GOOD.......VERY GOOD.......AMAZING......YOU MOST ADMIRE........12

- In each box next to the question symbol, write in colour the number value you have about the 8 qualities you most admire in others.
- In the question symbol draw <u>your personal symbol</u> that reflects the word.
- Draw some more symbol qualities you admire in others.

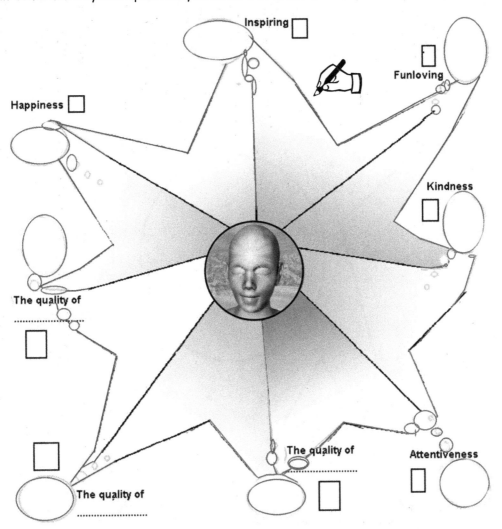

The Psychic Channel where ideas are Born

Fourth exercise on a mundane level

Many of us seem to have an admiration, or have an inner wish when we were still in school, what job or occupation we would like to apply or study for. Most people end up in completely different jobs or occupations in the end.

Guidelines:

What format and which colour triggers feelings you have surrounding jobs or <u>occupations</u>

When you think back about your aspirations and what feelings you still have surrounding them, mentally travel within and explore <u>through your 5 senses</u> which format inspires you the most when you think of those dreams long gone, and which colour guides you.

• Observe how each format affects your thoughts as you colour them in. Write in a few words what came up for you.
....

Level One/ Stage One 55

Any Idea that will inspire your Conscious mind

Fourth exercise on a soul level

Guidelines:

1.........NEAT........GOOD........VERY GOOD........AMAZING.......YOU MOST ASPIRE TO........12

- In each box next to the question symbol, write in colour the numeral value you have about the 8 occupations or directions people take on in their lives.
- In the box that says 'My idea' draw in your own numeral value surrounding your idea.

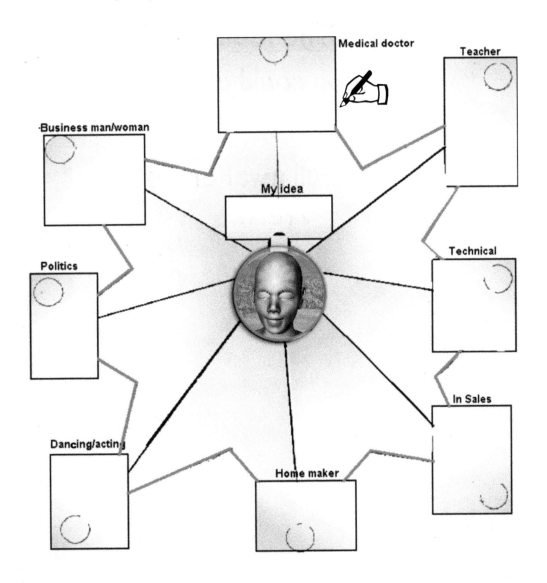

The tools
you could use
for
your full awakening
are....

Your Chakra cards

These cards will show to you how, your awareness level within the illusion of this dream manifest your realities.

Your Language of Light cards

These cards will activate more psychic energy within your auric field in order to fully awaken from this dream.

Your Five Elemental cards

These cards are your observation tools by which you can make an assessment on your ascension journey.

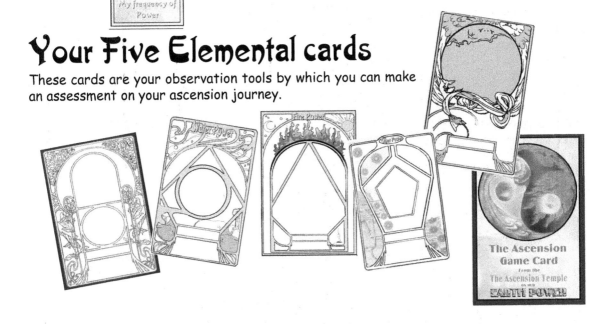

The 1st Language of Light Quality
Your symbol of Forgiveness

Forgiveness is the leader vibration of the Language of Light. In order to add more energy of light into our physical form we need to embody the qualities of our Soul. This language of light vibration brings the gift of change. When we embrace this quality we will have the determination to pursue our soul purpose or our visions in order to manifest them into physical form. Every soul that has the intent to awaken to full consciousness in this incarnation must fully embody the frequency of forgiveness.

Guidelines

During our following mind-drawing exercise we do an assessment and gather information from our energy field.

- First we address the 'body avatar' to assist us in this exercise..
- Which event(s) of your life can you still find it difficult to apply total forgiveness?
- As you contemplate this question, travel through your energy field and become aware of thought-forms that still hold feelings that need to be healed and forgiven.
- While you listen to your inner guidance. Take your drawing tools and draw in the circle, in an analogue way, the feelings that you now release.

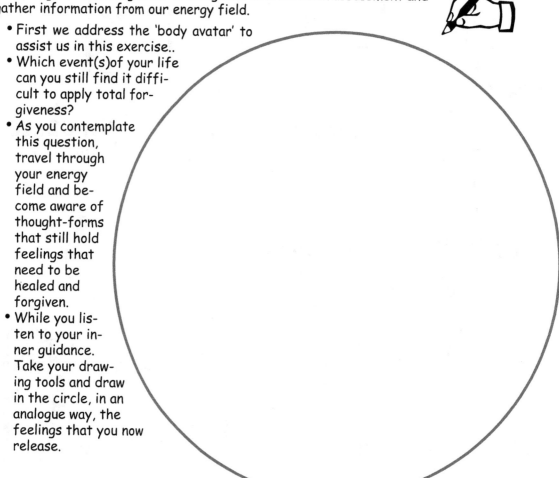

Level One / Stage One 59

Your Language of Light Card of Forgiveness

Draw your final symbol of forgiveness in the circle within your card. This 1st frequency of the soul carries the gift of change, determination and for some leadership qualities. This forgiveness vibration stimulates our visions to manifest our wishes into form.

Tip

Have two colour copies made of your first Language of Light card, reduce it to a business card size. Paste one in your Language of Light card at the back of the workbook in the booklet section. And laminate the other

The Base Chakra: your instinctual mind channel

With the symbol of Forgiveness

This first consciousness centre is mainly preoccupied with food, shelter or whatever we associate with our personal security. The lesson in this vortex is to release the need to get 'enough' in order to feel secure.

On your right you see 6 Language of Light frequencies that can be embodied through the Base Chakra.

- The **1st** frequency carries the gift of change, determination, leadership qualities, making visions manifest into form and of **forgiveness**
- The **10th** frequency **peaceful bliss** comes into action if all the 5 octaves are embodied for the purpose of awakening those with soul agreements to become the leaders of tomorrow.
- The **19**th octave of **perseverance** brings an awareness that focus and dedication to live one's soul purpose will inspire in others unity consciousness.

- The frequency of the **28**th octave is the gift of knowledge that divine union in action will bring forth the memory of one's soul **purpose**.
- In our **friendships** with others this **37**th frequency will awaken in ourselves and others the remembrance of true freedom..
- This **46**th frequency can only flourish when we have gone beyond the co-dependent patterns of love and move into the unconditional independence of ourselves and others.
- This **46**th quality will bring about **global unity**.

Level One / Stage One 61

Your Base Chakra Card

Draw and colour in your final Base Chakra card. Add your first language of Light Symbol and colour in the rest of the five circles.

Tip

When you have finished, have two colour copies made of your first Base Chakra card, reduce it to a business card size. Paste one in your Base card at the back of the workbook in the booklet section. And laminate the other

Your First insight

On the First Creative Stage Surrounding your Idea.

- In this 'closure' exercise on; <u>The First Creative Stage</u> we draw our Art-analogue Symbolism expression of our <u>first insight.</u>
  - This can be an insight into ourselves to do with a sudden awareness of a new idea on the mundane level.
  - Or this can also be a shift of perception to do with our relationships, work, interest, or what we have to do in order to manifest a new direction in our lives.
- This first insight mind-drawing reveals what you have gained throughout this first level called: <u>The desire to become aware.</u>

- Observe if your first insight comes from the past, at this moment, or from your future visions?
- Observe which of the seven chakra channels was the most active throughout this first level?
- Observe your physical, emotional, mental and your intuitive/creative awareness levels during this art-analogue mind-drawing.
- Make a note by writing in a few words what your feelings are surrounding your first insight after your mind-drawing exercise.

Your First Insight 63

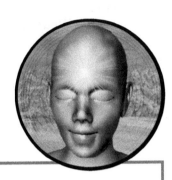

64 The Language of Light

Make notes on this page surrounding your idea. During the first stage you have focussed on an idea. This can be a new job, a new relationship, a different location to live, a new business etc..
Write down what has come up for you during the first stage of creativity surrounding an idea on a mundane level.

On a soul level write down what has come up for you regarding your soul's passion. What activity gives you great joy.

The Second Stage

Where your <u>ideas are investigated</u>
* The energy field of your Base Chakra.
* Our logical and Literal Mind
  * We are gathering more information
  * A mandala about your emotional expressions
* The <u>Sacral Chakra card</u> (your sensation centre)
* Our Language of Light Symbol that reflects <u>'Structure'</u>
* The energy field of your <u>Sacral Charkra</u>
* The <u>Solar Plexus card</u> (your power centre)
  * The Nine Masks we wear
* The <u>Solar Plexus</u> with the Language of Light Qualities
* Your Second insight.

66 The Language of Light

Your Base Chakra's Energy Field
The First energy channel that energises the physical body through the Red ray

A lot can be read from our first mind-drawing exercises when we study our hidden security and fear drawings. Look at the colours you have chosen for the things you rate highly. An inner language starts to form. The colour vibrations that are created by our thoughts are in a constant movement in our auric energy field. The speed of our vibrations on a cellular level influences the material world we perceive.

Study the Base Chakra field diagram and then go back to your previous mind drawings. If one's <u>fear</u> of living to one's fullest potential is held within the Base Chakra (located at the base of the spine), that fear energy surrounds all our survival issues.

These dysfunctional energy pockets within our energy field often manifest in the desire or the belief that the "grass is greener" someplace else. The thought "if only I lived at the sea, I'd be happy" is the sign of a first chakra that is in turmoil. The first chakra is related to the first Red ray which gives "birth" to life.

The Red ray governs our pioneers who forge ahead and create new pathways and invent new technology. Within the opposite polarity of this ray, an individual can become a hermit who lives in fear of everyone and everything.

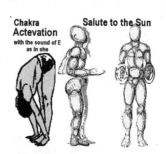
Chakra Actevation with the sound of E as in she   Salute to the Sun

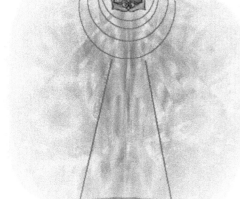

The gift of the first chakra the gift of living in the moment in total joy with whatever you are doing, and whomever you are with.

Those gifted with all the **six** Language of Light qualities in their first energy field will bring forth a new civilization upon Earth by forging ahead with new technology or restructuring old systems to fit a new fifth-dimension- al paradigm.

The First Pathway for your Soul.

The first energy channel that energises the physical body through the Red ray

During the exercise below practise standing away from yourself and become your observer that is looking at your auric field.

Fill the information that you gathered from the previous mind-drawing exercises and draw them in the energy field of the Base Chakra.

Take the numbers from your four security, fear based, admire and inspire drawings and place them in their circles.

Study the colours you have chosen for the numbers. Observe your thoughts as you do the drawing. If you want to release some thought forms that you don't want to hang on to, release them by sending then away to be transformed as you re-draw their symbols or colours.

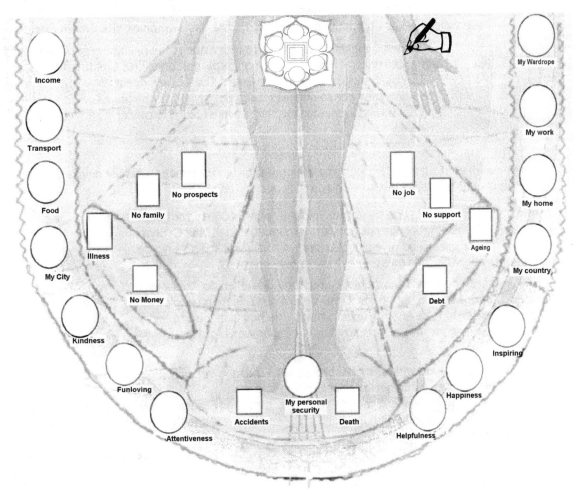

Your Logical and Literal Mind

Where your ideas are investigated

On the second level of our awakening our logical left brain hemisphere thinking mode merges with the richness of our right hemisphere mode of thinking on a day to day basis. Throughout this workbook we associate this awareness level with both our Sacral and Solar Plexus chakra. Most of our daily thoughts stream through these two conscious awareness levels at the beginning of our investigation surrounding our idea.

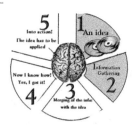

Our Logical thinking mind flows through the Sacral Chakra, on a mundane level with the assistance of our unconventional mind that flows through the Third Eye Chakra on a Soul level. At a later stage on this second conscious awareness level, our thoughts gradually flow through our Solar Plexus on a mundane level with the assistance of the Crown Chakra.

- Richard Jaarsma was asked to write about his dreaming experiences in his journals titled:'The Astral Explorer and The Cosmic Traveller'. It was from him, that I learned the art of dreaming. He made me aware that consciousness does not think, it conceives.
- POWAH also reminded me that we must learn to conceive instead of merely thinking.

It's during our dream time or through these mind-drawing exercises that we awaken the Language of light qualities that vibrate on that frequency level

From our Sacral chakra energy vortex, most of our thoughts that deal with sensational issues from our past or future, flow through this Orange The colours yellow, green and blue are also seen in this vortex. This energy is also an outgoing vibration mostly related to our emotions.

POWAH mentioned that inorganic beings are addicted to this emotional energy and that we meet them in our dream time. Richard explained how he interprets them during his dream time. (He has managed to move his conscious awareness into his energy body, his body of Light.)

- On the right page you will see five boxes with a space for writing. In this mind-drawing exercise we gather information surrounding our ideas.
- Before you start, prepare a music with five different music tunes on a CD. The music pieces have to be around 5 min long and they must have a break of silence before a different piece of music is heard.
- Each music piece must be totally different, from a classical piece, to rock, to a quick beat, to a meditative sound back to another classical tune.

Your Logical and Literal Mind　Level Two / Stage Two　69

Rapid drawing through Music.

The next three exercises are all accessed from our mundane level

- Draw out through line and movement how your thinking mode appears in colour, shape or symbol

First music piece

Second music piece

Third music piece

Fourth music piece

The Fifth music piece

- Write a feeling word below each box directly during the silence part.

- On the next two pages follow the same way but instead of the 5x 5 min music pieces make and play 12 pieces of music of approx.2 minutes long with a 1 min break in between that reflect the mood of the words.
- This tape will be approximately 30 min on each side.

The Mandala of your Emotional Expressions

Remember that your future is: any past memory that is still effective enough to impulse your behaviour now.

- Be in your body and feel the colours, line and texture flow from your hand onto the paper.

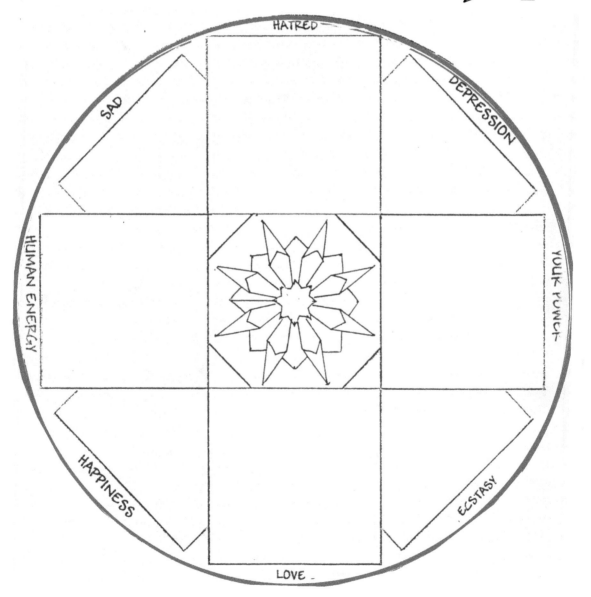

Level Two / Stage Two 71

The Mandala of your Emotional Expressions

Remember that your future is: any intent to awaken to full consciousness that your emotional expression <u>now</u> reflects.

- Both your emotionally expressed mind-drawings most be done honestly and sincerely.

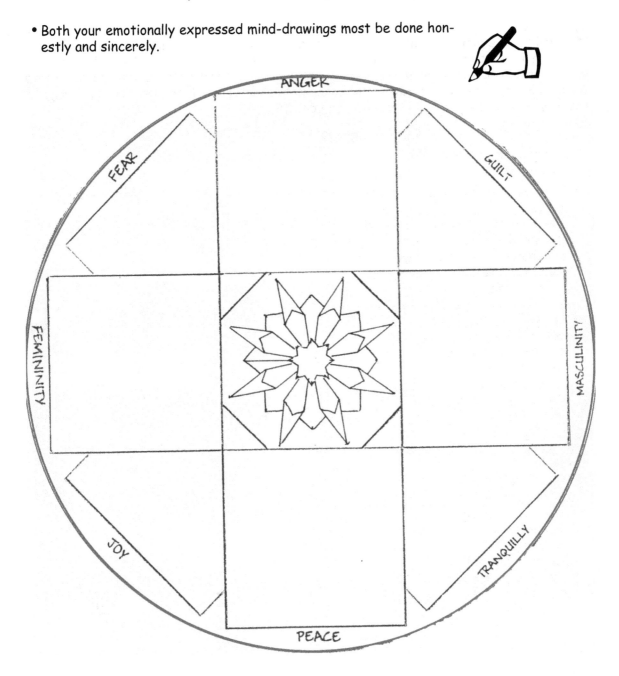

Your 2nd Language of Light Quality

Your symbol for Structure

Structure is the gift of this second chakra. This energy channel surrounds emotions and sexuality. The gift inherent within this chakra is governed by the second Orange/Scarlet ray which gives 'structure' to life. Second ray individuals are those who are helpful in maintaining structure, such as accountants, attorneys, or governmental agencies. The pelvis of both the masculine and feminine form has the capacity to channel very high vibrations of energy for the purposes of leadership, governance, and creation.

Guidelines

During the following mind-drawing exercise we do an assessment and gather information from our energy field.

- First we address the 'body avatar' to assist us in this exercise..
- Which event(s) in your life can you still say that there is a lack of structure? This gift is earned when our emotions, which are connected with your sexuality, is in balance.
- As you contemplate this question, travel through your energy field and become aware of thought-forms that still hold fear surrounding sexuality in your life.
- While you listen to your inner guidance take your drawing tools and draw in the circle, in an analogue way, the feelings that you now release surrounding a lack of structure.

Level Two / Stage Two 73

Your Language of Light Card of <u>Structure</u>

Draw your final symbol of Structure in the circle within your card. This 2nd frequency of the soul carries the gift of manifestation or creation.

When you have finished, have two colour copies made of your second Language of Light card, reduce it to a business card size. Paste one in your Language of Light card at the back of the workbook in the booklet section. And laminate the

The Sacral Chakra: our emotional intelligence

With your symbol of Structure

The sacral/sexual chakra represents our sensation centre. This vortex sits in front in the pelvic area and corresponds to the reproductive and urinary systems. It governs sexuality and emotions. This centre is concerned with finding happiness in life by providing ourselves with more and better pleasurable sensations and activities. This chakra is often closed or damaged in one who is either overly emotional or sexual, or the polar opposite of total repression or frigidity.

On your right you see 6 Language of Light frequencies that can be embodied through the Sacral Chakra

- The **2nd** frequency carries the gift of focus, compassion, commitment and stability, qualities making visions manifest into <u>structures</u>.
- This **11th** frequency brings the information on ascension to the conscious attention of the person in order to show a <u>direction</u>.
- The **20th** tonal frequency brings forth <u>hidden knowledge</u> within any teacher of universal truth in order to guide others on their path.

- The **29th** frequency adds <u>integrity</u> to the teacher of truth in order to acknowledge the divinity in everyone that crosses one's path.
- The **38th** tonal frequency brings the quality of knowing how to apply the right use of power through <u>communion.</u>
- This **47th** frequency bathes the awakened person with the vibrations of harmony, union, unity and <u>divine union</u> in order to love humanity.

Level Two / Stage Two 75

Your Sacral Chakra Card

Draw and colour in your final Sacral Chakra card. Add your second language of Light Symbol and colour the rest of the five circles.

Tip

When you have finished, have two colour copies made of your first Sacral Chakra card, reduce it to a business card size. Paste one in your Sacral chakra in the booklet section and laminate the other

76 The Language of Light

Your Second insight

On the second Creative Stage Surrounding your Idea.

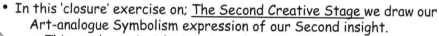

- In this 'closure' exercise on; <u>The Second Creative Stage</u> we draw our Art-analogue Symbolism expression of our Second insight.
  - This can be an insight into ourselves to do with a sudden awareness of a new idea on the mundane level.
  - Or this can also be a shift of perception to do with our relationships, work, interest, or what we have to do in order to manifest a new direction in our lives.
- This Second insight mind-drawing reveals what you have gained throughout this first level called: To become aware that we are unaware.

- Observe if your second insight comes from the past, present, or from your future visions.
- Observe which of the seven chakra channels was the most active throughout this second level.
- Observe your physical, emotional, mental and your intuitive/creative awareness levels during this art-analogue mind-drawing.
- Make a note by writing in a few words what your feelings are surrounding your second insight after your mind-drawing exercise on the second level.

Your Second insight 77

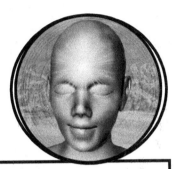

78 The Language of Light

Make notes on this page surrounding your information on your idea. During this second stage you have focussed on what it takes to manifest your idea On this stage you have gathered information surrounding your idea.

Write down what has come up for you during the Second stage of creativity surrounding an idea on a mundane level.

On a soul level write down what has come up for you regarding your soul's passion. What activity gives you great joy. What information has come your way that had to do with your idea.

....
....
....
....
....
....
....
....
....
....
....
....
....
....
....
....

The Third Stage

__Where your ideas are explored through action!__

* The energy field of your Sacral chakra.
  * The Nine masks we wear
* The Language of light card (your inner power)
* The Solar Plexus card
  * The Perception we have of ourselves
* The energy field of your Solar Plexus
  * Your body Language
* The Bridge across forever.
* The Language of light card (of compassion)
* The Heart Chakra
* Your Third insight

Your Sacral Chakra's Energy field
The Second channel that energises the physical body through the orange/Scarlet Ray

When we recollect the mind-drawings on the second level, most of our thoughts that deal with sensational issues from our past or future are often expressed through bright colours. The brighter the colours gives us an indication that we:
- Loosen up while drawing because this energy is an outgoing vibration related to our emotions.
- It reveals that you could very well have a very active Sacral chakra.

When I wrote about inorganic beings, see them as energy entities that are actually thought-forms that were left behind in our third-dimensional realm by:
- Our (genetic) ancestors of long past.
- Ascended beings that left them behind with their devotees!
- Souls that fell so low in consciousness due to the incompatibility with our universe.
- Our own Oversoul; they are our own soul particles that we dumped into other soul mates during other embodiments.

(See page 246 The law of Karma)
- Illuminati (See index)
- Implantation.(See index)
- By Maldek..during our dream-time. (See page 246 on the law of Karma)

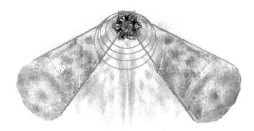

Salute to the Sun
with the sound of i as in ice

Remember!
Nobody is without distorted energy particles in their energy field. It's just another way of interpreting Karma.
See page 246 On the law of Karma

The Second Pathway of your Soul

The Second channel that energises the physical body through the orange/Scarlet Ray

Again a lot can already be cleared from the mind-drawing exercises that influence our emotional intelligence. In this energy field, look at the colours you have chosen for the things you rate highly, or you still have a strong reactive energy level to. Fill your information from the previous exercises in the Sacral Chakra energy field. Use the numbers next to your Mandala of your emotional expression and transfer the colours, shapes, lines or symbols in their appropriate spacings in your Sacral Chakra energy field.

Feel if there still could be any blockages in this energy region.

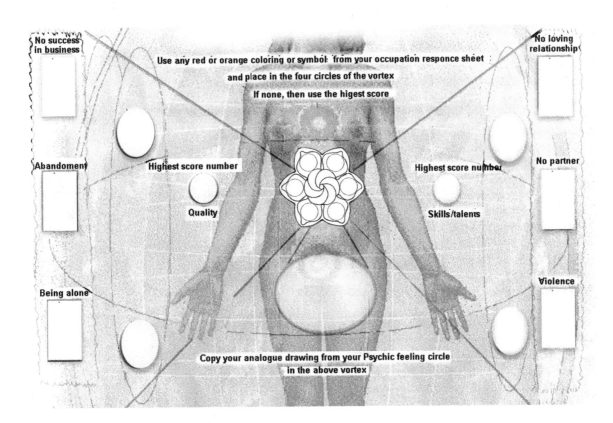

The Nine Masks You Wear

Within the dream of reality you are the observer of your dream

The illusion of our reality is continually established through the beliefs we hold on to. We live in our own virtual reality show, and some will even die for it! We are so attached to our self image in this reality, that is what keeps us in the dark as to who we really are. We do this through the many masks we wear. The masks we wear are like inorganic beings (our personas) who use every opportunity to jump on the stage to act out yet another character. How many characters do we project out there?

Annelies, POWAH and later Richard were my best teachers when they explained, each in their own way, how the mind-drawing exercises shifted their perceptions. I discovered that the exercises that I tried out on people had a much more profound meaning behind them. Someone was watching! As you draw your masks, feel the being(s) that are watching over your shoulder while you draw.

I myself was just as blind to the dynamics of the exercises. I know that while my participants were drawing, in those moments their observer must have become aware of energies our five physical senses are fooled by. The moment you observe your 'masks' you become aware of inorganic beings that whisper in your ear to keep you in the dark. You will also become aware that we have all been unaware.

Guidelines
- For every format you have 2 minutes! What does your mask look like through.....
- 1. In the Pentagon format draw the mask you wear for your close family.
- 2. In the Star format draw the mask you see in the mirror each morning.
- 3. In the Diamond format draw the mask you wear in front of an intimate friend.
- 4. In this Pentagon draw the mask you wear for your colleagues.
- 5. In the Square format draw the mask you wear for your good friends.
- 6. In the Circle draw the mask you wear for your relatives.
- 7. In the Triangle draw the mask you wear for authority.
- 8. In the Hexahedron draw the mask you wear for your acquaintances.
- 9. In the last Triangle draw the mask you wear for beggars, hoboes or persistent salesmen.

Stage Three / Level Three 83

We are all actors on a stage

Be totally honest and become your own observer. Take your non-dominant hand and draw in an analog, or in a symbolic way what face you show to the outside world. Most of us wear different masks for different occasions.

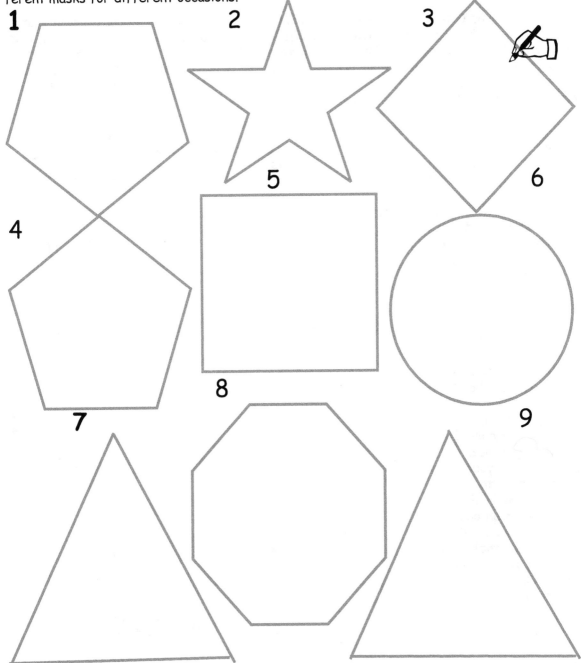

Your 3rd Language of Light Quality
Your symbol of Inner Power

The vibration of Inner Power is the gift of this third chakra. This vortex controls our status and the ego. This is also the area where excitement of life as well as our fears are felt. It is located at the level of the navel. This vortex is the subtle centre that influences the activities of digestion and absorption of food. This is the chakra that 'when damaged' we are a slave to our ego. Physical problems in the solar plexus area can therefore relate to the conflict of power and ego-identity issues, represented by this chakra.

Guidelines

During the following mind-drawing exercise we do an assessment and gather information from our previous two insights.

- First we again address the 'body avatar' to assist us in this exercise..
- Which event(s) of your life can you still find it difficult to apply your inner power to. As you contemplate this question, travel through your energy field and become aware of thought-forms that still hold feelings that need to be healed.
- While you listen to your inner guidance. take your drawing tools and draw in the circle, in an analogue way, the feelings that you now release in order to access your inner power.

Your Language of Light Card of Inner Power

Draw your final symbol of your Inner power Language of Light drawing in the circle within your card. This 3rd frequency of the soul stimulates our visions and gives us energy and strength to manifest our wishes into form.

Tip

When you have finished, have two colour copies made of your third Language of Light card, reduce it to a business card size. Paste one in your Language of Light card at the back of the workbook in the booklet section. And laminate the other

The Solar Plexus: your questioning mind

Your lower mental intelligence where your ideas are further explored

This centre is mainly preoccupied with power issues. The gift inherent within the third chakra is the right use of power, which is power based on unconditional love. Those embodying the right use of power are our future leaders who will govern large bodies of people, nations or organizations, based upon unconditional love and collaboration. The lesson in this vortex is to recognise that we have an internal world that reflects our external world. This third awareness level is guided by the orange/yellow ray. The colour yellow is associated with the adrenal glands.

On your right you see 6 Language of Light frequencies that can be embodied through the Solar Plexus chakra.

- The **3**rd frequency carries the gift of <u>inner power</u>
- This **12**th frequency brings <u>hope</u> to all who have a desire to become aware.
- This **21**st tonal frequency prepares anyone who aspires to become a world teacher. Consciousness is raised through the quality of <u>creativity.</u>
- The **30**th frequency adds <u>balance</u> to the teacher of truth. They know that true creativity heals everyone that crosses one's path.
- This **39**th tonal frequency brings true creativity to one's union with the divine. It will heighten anyone's <u>dance of life</u> through meditation.
- This **48**th frequency stimulates the vibrations of harmony and union so that the <u>god/goddess</u> within can start to bring love to humanity

Your Solar Plexus Chakra Card

Draw and colour in your Solar Plexus Chakra card. Add your third Language of Light Symbol of your Inner power and colour in the rest of the five Language of Light quality circles.

Tip

When you have finished, have two colour copies made of your Solar Plexus Chakra card, reduce it to a business card size. Paste one card at the back of the workbook in the booklet section. And laminate the other.

The Perception we have of Ourselves

The twelve directions of my awareness centres

- The following 12 questions must be answered in all honesty through your feeling nature in order to be of any value to you. How we truly feel about ourselves is often exposed through the following questions in this mandala.
- In an analogue way go within and feel how your body responds to the words. <u>Be in your body!</u>
- The break between the 12 pieces of music played in the background will guide you when to move to the next question. (Have a tape ready)
- Start at the top with number 1 and go clockwise and become your own observer.

- 1 How do I feel about my life right now?
- 2 Do I like myself?
- 3 How do I feel about my body?
- 4 How do I feel about sex?
- 5 How do I feel about my home?
- 6 How do I feel about my job/career?
- 7 How do I feel about my partner or close family?
- 8 How do I feel about my failures?
- 9 How do I feel about change?
- 10 How do I feel about my future?
- 11 Who am I really?

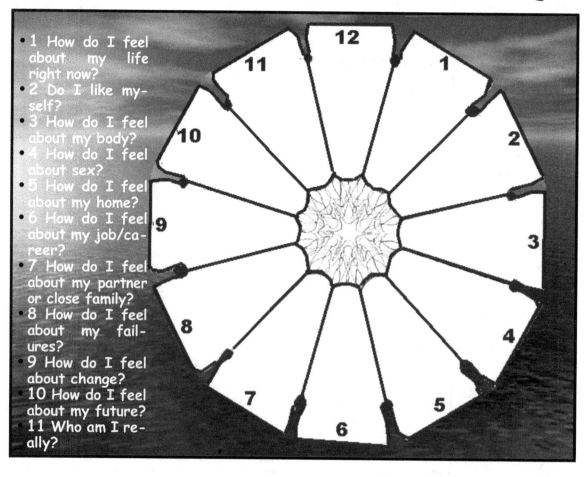

Level Three / Stage Three 89

The Mandala of Your Social self

And the universe around me

We are all energy beings. We could just as well have chosen to experience being a tree, or a flower or any other creator that walks on this planet but we did not. We chose to explore what it is like to be creators of worlds and how to maintain the illusion of this world. During the experiment we fell into a massive amnesia. We became trapped in our own dream. We even created a portal to get out of this reality during certain times, but most of the time we just became the dreamer roaming around our own energy field re-creating our own reality in an ever more distorted way.

In the format below I want you to explore how the world looks like to you in the media of colour. What does your dream world looks like. How are you coping in this world to do with your <u>inner power</u>.

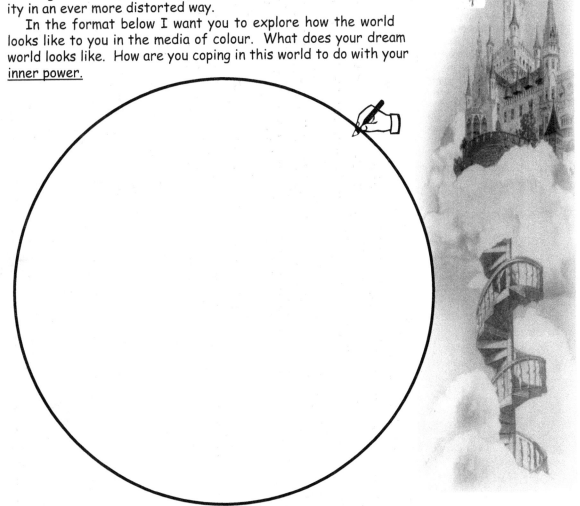

Your Body Language

Your Sad face

Get a mirror and place it in front of you. Self reflection is often quite uncomfortable but revealing. Look at yourself in the mirror as you think of something that makes you sad, worried or angry.

Observe what feelings come up and draw them out in any way you like. You may draw your portrait, or just an analogue expression of the feelings you feel.

Be spontaneous and number your feelings about them within the blocks next to your drawing and give them a feeling word.
- Number the message level from 1—12 what thoughts are coming up for you?
- How would those facial expressions prevent you from experiencing your ideas?

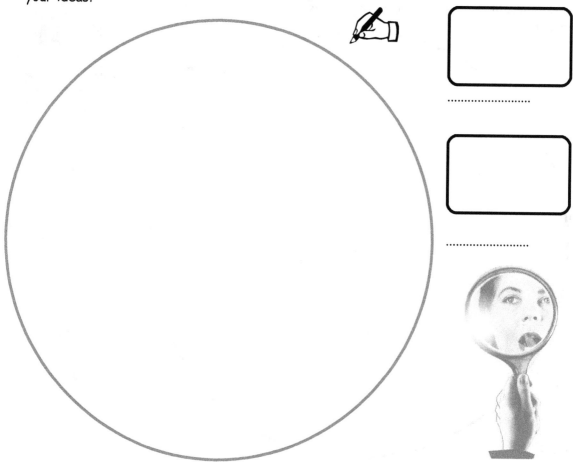

Your Body Language

Your Happy face

Our body language is often the most revealing message others perceive us by. How our body language comes across can sometimes completely wipe away any authenticity surrounding our spoken words. Our Solar Plexus channel is often in stress as we feel we have to create an image, when we have to deal with our world. The pain in our naval region does not come from any organs or what we have eaten, it's our Solar Plexus that is trying to hold on to our inner power.

On this consciousness level we are often shattered by others who try to control us or have us do things we don't want to do. Many people lose or have lost their inner power through this energy channel to others.

- As you do this drawing, <u>take back</u> the inner power you might have lost.
- Observe how your happy smile gives you back the strength you always had.

Your Solar Plexus chakra's Energy field
The third channel that energises the physical body through the Orange/Scarlet ray

When we recollect the mind-drawings on the third level, most of our thoughts that deal with power and control issues from our past or future are expressed through movement and texture in our drawings. The stronger the art-work comes across, the stronger our issues that surrounds control have an impact on our lives.

This energy channel is often damaged in a person who fluctuates between being either overly controlling in a situation, and then quickly relinquishing control when things do not work out. Manipulation and subversive behaviour patterns are often part of this particular consciousness level. When we are out of balance on this level we are either overly emotional and sexual to needy, or the polar opposite of total repression or frigidity is displayed.

Annelies helped me a great deal when she pointed out that my partner had dumped his emotional body on me, when I allowed him to take my inner power. Through my own manipulation tendencies for self survival I took his mental body during the time of our separation. This was not allowed and the result was that he had a heart attack. I needed to help him get back to health before I could be free to follow my own path.

'The Awakening Clan"

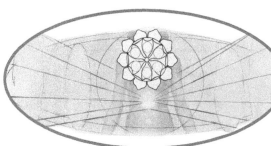

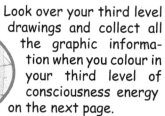

Look over your third level drawings and collect all the graphic information when you colour in your third level of consciousness energy on the next page.

Your Solar Plexus chakra's Energy field
The Third energy channel that energises the physical body through the Orange/Scarlet ray

This energy channel is also the Major antenna of our body when it comes to picking up moods and feelings that other people express without mentioning them.

For example when we walk in a room and we suddenly feel welcome or unwelcome. Or we visit a public place where an argument is taking place. Many people feel the emotion that is flying around and walk away.

Some people can't stop themselves for <u>not</u> getting involved. Those people are usually totally unaware that they are being used as a dumping vessel for distorted energies. But then, through this energy channel we often deal with unresolved issues from our Sacral chakra. So who knows, by getting mixed up with other people's drama, we heal our own.

When you are focussed on this energy centre, feel how you body responds to your every thought. 'Worry' is poisonous energy to this chakra and laughter is the healing tonic. As you colour your solar plexus' energy field, think back on the exercises that deal with our self-image.

Visualise that a beam of light is entering into your Solar Plexus, spreading light particles in all directions. Channel any disjointed thought forms you are ready to release into this beam of light.

94 The language of Light

The Bridge across forever...
Awakens..

..your higher mind...
    Where compassion for all life…
Will influence our co-creative choices…
    As we move Into a new paradigm.
        Towards a different dream.

Your 4th Language of Light Quality
Your symbol for Compassion

Compassion is the Language of Light quality on this fourth consciousness level. The fourth chakra is governed by the fourth ray, which is green in colour, which gives "harmony to life." Fourth ray individuals are our healers, doctors, and our medicine men and women. The gift inherent within the fourth chakra is the gift of love. Ingrid and Toon are examples of a couple relationship between equal partners that embrace and educate others in a fifth-dimensional paradigm for marriage, family, and divine union.

During this mind-drawing exercise we do an assessment and gather all the information from our previous mind-drawings.
- Again we address the 'body avatar' to assist us in this exercise.
- Which event(s) of your life can you still find it difficult to apply compassion to your life? This gift is only earned when our Heart charka is opened.
- Often it's activated due to a wake-up call.
- Most of you who know what I'm talking about will recall how much easier it was to feel compassion for others if you've been there, yourself.
- As you contemplate this question, feel your body and become aware of thought-forms that still lack compassion in your life.
- While you listen to your inner guidance, take your drawing tools and draw in the circle, in an analogue way, the feelings that you now release surrounding a lack of compassion.

Level Three / Stage Three 97

Your Language of Light Card of <u>Compassion</u>

Draw your symbol of Compassion in the circle within your Symbol of light card.

This 4th frequency of the soul carries the gift of love for all life. This loving vibration will stimulate and nurture our visions to manifest our dreams into manifestations.

Tip

When you have finished, have two colour copies made of your fourth Language of Light card, reduce it to a business card size. Paste one in your Language of Light card at the back of the workbook in the booklet section. And laminate the other

The Heart Chakra: your holistic mind channel

With the symbol of Compassion

We have reached the fourth centre where 'work' is no longer performed unconsciously or mechanically. Our feeling nature is preparing us for a new energy flow which will increase our growth into higher consciousness. The Heart centre is our most important vortex. Its 12 petals surround the 10 frequencies of the Language of Light form the threshold towards higher consciousness. This vortex must be fully activated if we want to transcend our security, sensation and power addictions. It is through this vortex that we learn to embrace all life with love.

- This **4**th frequency carries the quality of <u>Compassion</u>. When the heart opens we see life with a flowing acceptance
- The strong frequency of the **8**th octave awakens the quality of <u>divine union</u> within the self, the universal spirit our group soul is calling us home.
- The **13**th frequency, when embodied, brings an <u>inner peace.</u>

- This **17**th frequency activates our <u>intuitive</u>/creative body to the full.
- Our natural, original <u>full awareness</u> will awaken with the **22nd numeral frequency**.
- This **26**th frequency brings you into <u>action</u> in order to transcend subject-object relationships.
- The quality of <u>Honour</u> is embodied through this **31st frequency**.
- This powerful **35th** octave brings our <u>creativity</u> out in the open.
- The **40**th frequency opens the heart to embrace everyone as being a gift to our community.
- The numeral frequency of the **44th** frequency reveals the often <u>hidden worlds</u> that were never spoke about.

Level Three / Stage Three 99

Your Heart Chakra Card

While you feel the love pouring into your whole being, draw and colour in your Heart Chakra card. Add your Language of Light Symbol of compassion and colour the rest of the other five Language of Light circles.

Tip

When you have finished, have two colour copies made of your Heart Chakra card, reduce it to a business card size. Paste one in the back of the workbook (in the booklet section). And laminate the other

Your Third insight

On the Third Creative Stage Surrounding your Idea.

- In this 'closure' exercise on; <u>The Third Creative Stage</u> we draw our Art-analogue Symbolism expression of our third insight.
- From this level onwards your awakening energy starts to create an effect on our lives. This stage is all around the most difficult level to be in. On the mundane level, the ideas we are exploring can sometimes experience great obstacles and we go through major changes. If it is to do with our relationships, often on this level we become aware with whom we have to break energy cords in order to honour ourselves.
- This is the level where most of us go through the dark night of the soul.

Now that we have passed the bridge of no return means that from this level onwards, we are fully responsible for every manifestation in our lives. From this level we will stop <u>blaming</u> unfortunate events on others. What is in our reality, we manifested to observe. We did not always create the difficulties ahead, but we choose to experience them. Many people on a spiritual path do not pass this level out of choice.

- Annelies warns people that when we make the intent to awaken to full consciousness, we have to be prepared to look at every aspect within ourselves. This can be very painful on the physical body as well as our mental, emotional and creative subtle bodies. At the interpretation section you can read about the body symptoms you can or might expect on this awakening journey,

Your Third insight 101

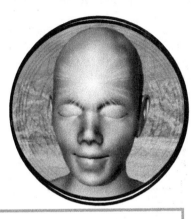

102 The Language of Light

Make notes on this page how you have applied your idea. During this third stage you have found out what it takes to manifest your idea On this stage you have experienced what obstacles are still in the way of your idea.
Write down what has come up for you during the third stage of creativity surrounding an idea on a mundane level.

On a soul level write down what has come up for you regarding your soul's passion and how much time you give to yourself. What activity gives you great joy. Which changes have come your way that had to do with your idea.

....

....

....

....

....

....

....

....

....

....

....

....

....

....

....

....

The Fourth Stage

Where your <u>ideas start to manifest</u>

* The energy field of your Heart chakra.
  * The gifts you bring into the world
  * The Mandala of your perception
  * Colour and your senses
* The <u>Throat Chakra</u>, (your abundance centre.)
  * The sound of your name.
* The <u>Throat Chakra</u> with the Language of Light Quality card
* Your fourth insight

Your Heart chakra's Energy field

The Fourth energy channel that energises the physical body through the Green ray

Some people call this energy layer of our auric field the Astral layer. Visualise a rainbow of colours that are all blending and dancing into each other. The first layer is our Etheric blueprint controlled by the Red ray.

The second layer (our emotional body) is controlled by the Orange to Scarlet ray. The third layer is controlled by the the yellow ray. Lots of yellow in an aura is seen with people who live in the head. It's our lower mental body.

People who have an active fourth Astral layer are infused with rose pink colours among the green. Especially when people are in love. When a relationship is causing great pain those people hold a lot of sadness around them, even if they are in denial. If one is sensitive enough you nevertheless know that something is not right. I experienced that with my daughter Hennie.

Annelies advised me not to do anything unless she would ask for it. Not a single person is aware enough to know what another soul wants to experience because we can't see the bigger picture.

From here on our body language is expressed through the Heart chakra. As soon as we open our perception on the fourth level we are starting to perceive people or beings who exist in the astral layers who don't have physical bodies.

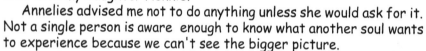

Salute to the Sun movement with the sound of A as in fate
Chakra Activation

Inorganic beings are mostly experienced in the first layer of the astral realm. They are eager to influence dreamers who are not aware.

Many people who hold powerful positions and are in stress are perfect targets. When Trevor speaks of the illuminates, believe me they are no joke! The hard part is that we created them!

Because the fourth level of consciousness deals with the energy of compassion, no judgmental thoughts can pass this realm. When our energy field is riddled with judgmental thoughts of any description we stay in the lower levels until we release them.

Your Fourth pathway of the Soul

The energy field of our Heart Chakra is very large. It permeates all the lower and the higher levels. This is often confusing when you start to see the energy fields around people. It's not all that easy to know what you are seeing.

People mistake the word seeing as if we see the energy field with the same visions as when we look at objects on this 3rd dimensional plane. When I started to recognise that I was seeing, I was surprised the way it came to me. Not anyway I thought. I remembered that as a child I saw the same thing but never realized that I saw something others did not see. Small children, animals especially cats, see into the same energy field. It's not all that special! You can even close your eyes and see!

When you do this mind-drawing, look into your inner vision. Allow the moving energies to float before you. Try not to analyse them. Learn to differentiate between your fantasy and inner visions.

Look back at the mind-drawing exercises you did on the third level to observe whether you have worked through some of your blockages.

Your Nine gifts that can enrich this reality

In order to know how we create our reality, draw out in a rapid way why you would pursue your idea or insight. Allow any shape to guide you. Notice which format triggers feelings of joy the most, surrounding your idea. In the wide box below express in an analogue way what support (or lack of) is there in order to manifest your idea.

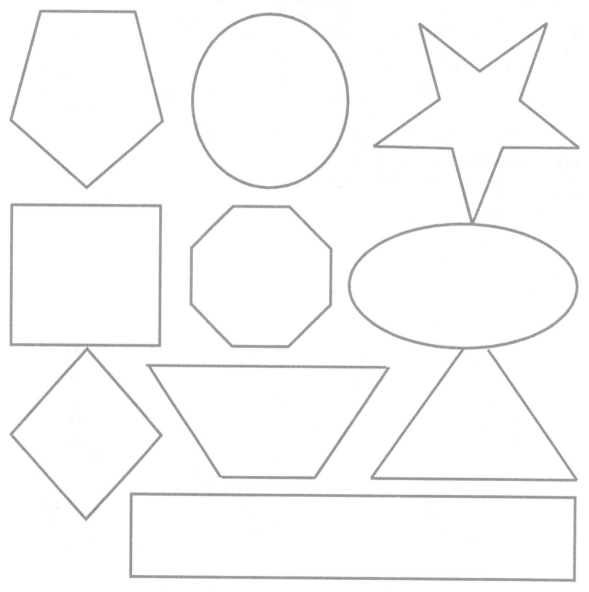

Your nine gifts that will bring joy to others
Express in an analogue way the energy you emanate to others

While we create our reality on a day to day basis by our thoughts, the joy we feel by just expanding on our idea, no matter how frivolous, will have an impact in our energy field. Visualisations and having an intent to pursue our dreams, no matter how unobtainable they might appear to be, is like food for the soul. During the years that I got to know Annelies, I was amazed at the nightmare she created for herself. I feel that many people would have opted out to the challenge she had to deal with.

Each person observes the world from an uniquely different angle and each person lives at a different manifestation speed.

That's right, we live in a world where our concept of <u>time</u> seems to control our manifestations, but this is an illusion. We can manipulate 'Time' to suit ourselves.

Some people seem to manifest their dreams a lot faster than others. Some people have no dream or have no awareness that they live in their own dream and that they are the dreamer. They just follow a certain programme that feels convertible and ask no questions.

They could be puppets to the 'inorganic beings' that use their energy in order to keep their reality in its place.

Not all obstacles on our path are a sign that we should not pursue our goals. In order to master the art of awakening to full consciousness and become co-creators in this reality, we need to have a lot of psychic energy. So we have to recognise the pitfalls that have deluded humanity for eons of time.

Colour and your Senses

Each of our five senses link up with a colour that triggers a feeling, which our brain translates into a symbolic shape. Most of these interactions are happening unconsciously. Our senses of smell, sight, touch, taste and hearing all enhance the experiences of the way we think.

In the following exercise we are intuitively linking our male and female energies in a way that can shed light on why we perceive and way we do.
- We do this by starting to merge our feelings with our senses in our physical associations to <u>food</u>.
- The chakra colours of Magenta, Violet, Dark Blue, Turquoise, Green, Yellow, Orange and Red are used during this exercise. (This workbook is published in a gray scale but an e-book version is available in full colour from Annelies' website: www.ascension-workshop.co.za)

Guidelines

- From the food chart on the next page study the foods that reflect your thoughts surrounding those chakra colours.
- Draw out four <u>feelings in the empty circle</u> that have suddenly sprung on you when you made a link between the food item and the chakra.

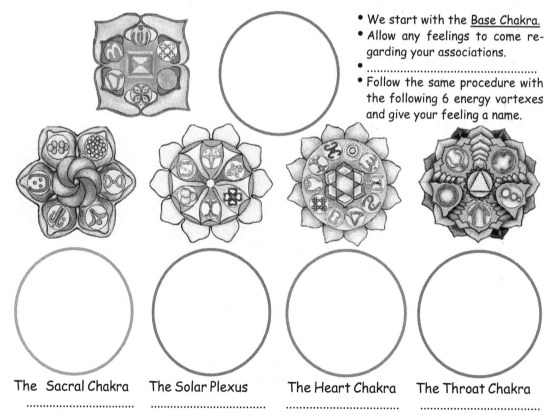

- We start with the <u>Base Chakra.</u>
- Allow any feelings to come regarding your associations.
- ....
- Follow the same procedure with the following 6 energy vortexes and give your feeling a name.

The Sacral Chakra
....

The Solar Plexus
....

The Heart Chakra
....

The Throat Chakra
....

Colour and your Senses

Food has to do with our survival, our well being, our attractions to taste, smell, texture, and sight. Food is a media we use to communicate through by sharing a meal, cooking for others and exchanging recipes. Food feeds our brain cells. There can be <u>no awakening</u> without food! A shortage of food in one's life has devastating effects on our existence whether we are aware of being in the dream or we are not!

Fasting is only partly beneficial under very special circumstances.

110 The Language of Light

The colour and your senses continued...

- First, colour the eight shapes on the right page from the top; Magenta, Violet, Dark Blue, Turquoise, Green, Yellow, Orange and Red and **choose 3 of your favourite colours** with their shapes and number them 1,2 and 3. Use the same colours but now draw them in the free form shape. (Notice if there is a change in your feelings)

The top **7**th is your <u>Crown</u> chakra that links your soul consciousness through the pineal gland with your eternal spiritual self. The energy of the colour Magenta, is a brilliant mauvish-crimson shade that connects you to an infinite intelligence. What kind of food did you relate to this colour in your drawings? ....

The **6**th vortex is Your <u>Third Eye</u> chakra that transmits your thought energy through your pituitary gland. What food items did you relate to the colour Violet in your drawings? ....

The **5**th vortex is your <u>Throat</u> chakra This is the centre of your creative expression. What food did you relate to the colour of Dark Blue in your drawings? ....

This in-between minor chakra with a <u>Turquoise</u> colour is very closely linked to the heart. It acts like a gateway into the higher levels of consciousness. What food item would you have related to this chakra in your drawings? ....

The **4**th vortex is our <u>Heart</u> chakra with the colour Green. This is the centre of love and harmony. Nature with our vegetables vibrates on the same wavelength. What food item did you relate to this chakra in your drawings? ....

The **3**rd vortex is our <u>Solar Plexus</u> chakra, like the sun its colour Yellow spreads great light to our nervous system. What food item did you relate to this chakra in your drawings? ....

The **2**nd vortex is the Orange/Scarlet <u>Sacral</u> energy chakra that relates to our adrenal glands. Through this Sacral Chakra our sense of well-being and joy connects us to the physical plane. What food did you relate to this chakra in your drawings? ....

The **1**st <u>Base Chakra</u> is connected with our passion for life and it stimulates the power to create. What or which type of food did you relate to the colour Red in your drawing? ....

Level Four/ Stage Four 111

The colour and your senses cont...
- Write or repeat your feeling word between the circle and the free form. Ask yourself what symbol, number or shape would you place into the circle that reflects your feelings for that colour.
- The reason for this rather involved exercise is to enhance your "A Ha" moment when you read up on your interpretations.

My first, second and third choice

Your 5th Language of Light Quality
The symbol the breath of Life

This Fifth ray's quality radiates outward when we connect through our communication skills. Synchronicity is starting to be a daily occurrence. This is the chakra that 'when damaged' people tell untruths or they have a fear that being honest to themselves will hurt others, so they rather hurt themselves by telling untruth. People who cannot express or communicate to others shut themselves off. Lack of abundance is then often triggered by the personality aspect that is locked in the Base Chakra's needs for feelings of being secure and in control. Most of us have hidden anguishes on different issues that can block our true abundance.

Guidelines

During this mind-drawing exercise we do an assessment and gather the information from our colour and our senses exercise. Again we address the 'body avatar' to assist us in this exercise.

- Which of the nine shapes from the previous exercise triggered the gift your idea brings into the world?
- Which (platonic) shape resonated the most for you?
- Which colour did you give it and which food item did you choose?
- Which chakra scored the highest number?
- As you contemplate the question above, feel your body and become aware of thought-forms that lack the breath of life.
- While you listen to your inner guidance, take your drawing tools and draw in the circle, in an analogue way, the feelings that for you reflects <u>Breath of life.</u>

Level Four/ Stage Four 113

Your Language of Light Card of the Breath of Life

Draw your symbol of the breath of life in the circle within your Symbol of light card. This 5th frequency of the soul carries the gift of speaking one's truth. This vibration stimulates our visions to manifest our abundance in life.

Tip

When you have finished, have two colour copies made of your fifth Language of Light card, reduce it to a business card size. Paste one in your Language of Light page at the back of the workbook in the booklet section. And laminate the other

The Throat Chakra: your abundance channel

With the symbol of the Breath of life

We have reached the fifth chakra which is associated with the cervical plexus, at the third cervical vertebra. This chakra influences our thyroid gland. This is our communication centre where the divine word is spoken through on the highest level from our higher self. It represents our state of awareness and openness to a deeper understanding of our self and our self-identity. It is also connected with our Base Chakra, which is where our personalities dwell. A well balanced person will blend their Red energy with the Blue in order to active Violet.

- The **5**th frequency is associated with <u>The Breath of Life</u>. This vibration brings the quality of purification into our spoken word. Our words become melodies that bring joy and peace into the world.
- The **14**th frequency of Abundance is activated when we know our soul purpose. Together with the 1st tonal energy of <u>Forgiveness</u> and the 10th gift of <u>Peaceful bliss</u>, prosperity is experienced on all levels.

- This **23**rd vibration brings the experience of Oneness into our lives when the quality of <u>Perseverance</u> 19 and 28 <u>Purpose</u> is embodied.
- The gift of the **32**nd vibration blends our Dream world with this physical life in order to embody more of our soul's energy force. We meet many soul mates and will experience true friendships when the vibration of 37 is embodied.
- The **41**st frequency of **Honesty** is embodied when we embrace the 46th energy of <u>Global Unity</u>.

Level Four/ Stage Four 115

The Throat Chakra Card

Draw and colour your Throat Chakra card. Any other numbers that came up in your previous exercises. Can be added to the chakra cards. Add your fifth language of Light Symbol in this card and colour the rest of the four circles, or leave them blank for later.

Tip

When you have finished, have two colour copies made of your fifth Throat Chakra card, reduce it to a business card size. Paste in one of your Throat chakra card at the back of the workbook in the booklet section. And laminate the other

Honour your Divine Within

This next exercise was especially created to see if people were really honouring themselves after doing all the mind-drawings. I collected some awesome mandala art-works over a period of time. Not one was the same but all had one thing in common. Every person that did this mandala on the next page loved the space the colouring in design created. We all love to escape into a world of kaleidoscopic splendour.

The twelve facets all have a special reason for being there. Take your time and be in your body when you draw your divine self through this mandala format.

Now is the time to look whether you are allowing yourself to receive the extraordinary gift of the Breath of Life.

If on the other hand you've been feeling despondent and the world is getting too much for you, take a break through simply being in the moment.

Be like a child and take your colour pencils and colour in your mandala.

Look at the 12 different shapes within the mandala and let your higher self do the doodling drawing.

Let your spirit free

It is time
to express
Yourself and Celebrate both the old and the coming of the new where the difference between Dreams and reality Is already known.

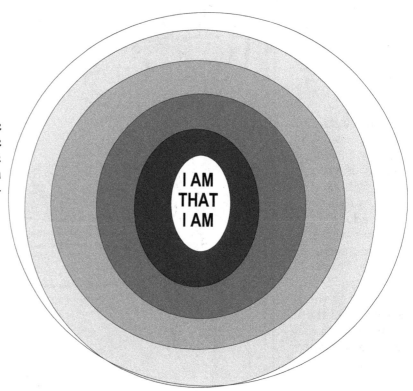

Level Four/ Stage Four 117

How awake are you?

My Air energy

My Earth energy

My Fire energy

My Water energy

Your Fourth insight

On the fourth Creative Stage Surrounding your Idea.

- This 'closure' exercise on; <u>The fourth Creative Stage,</u> our Art-analogue Symbolism expression of our fourth insight will take on a different approach. By now you will have experiences and some meaningful A ha moments. For some of you your <u>idea</u> has become concretized. You have taken action and have started to manifest the results.
- If your idea was a long term one you will by now be a lot clearer as to where to go from here.
- Whatever you do, if you do it joyfully, if your act of doing is not purely economical, then it is creative.
- When your creativity comes to a climax, your whole life becomes creative.

This illumination stage is often the most addictive of the levels of creativity. We love being on this level of our personal development. Many people become, what I call bliss-bunnies.

We can't stay on this level for very long. Now that we are presented with an opportunity to see life in all its dimensions, when we come to know from experience that the dark and the light moments in our lives are needed to shift our perspective on the world, we become more integrated.

Your Fourth Insight 119

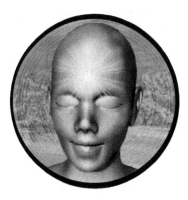

120 The Language of Light

Make notes on this page about what you have learned from your idea During this fourth stage you have had many moments of great insights surrounding your idea On this stage you have experienced what works and what does not.

Write down what has come up for you during the fourth stage of creativity surrounding an idea on a mundane level.

On a soul level write down what awakening insights are your experiencing on this fourth level. How often can you spend time on the activity that gives you great joy. What changes have you made in order to manifest your dream.

....

....

....

....

....

....

....

....

....

....

....

....

....

....

....

The Fifth Stage

Where your <u>ideas are manifested</u>

* The energy field of your Throat chakra.
  * The sound of your name
* The Third Eye with the Language of Light Qualities.
* The Third Eye Chakra (your conscious-awareness centre)
* The Crown Chakra with the Language of Light Qualities
* The energy field of your Third Eye
* The Crown Chakra card. (your unity consciousness centre)
  * The auric field of the real you
* Your Fifth insight.

Your Throat chakra's Energy field
The Fifth energy channel that energises the physical body through the blue/fuchsia ray

The **fifth chakra** is located within the neck area. The gift 'the Breath of Life' surrounds creativity and self-expression. This chakra often manifests its full creative self-expression, when the individual accomplishes great artistic feats, such as a novel, painting, or creative inventive ideas that make a difference to people's lives. The lack of this gift manifests the opposite extreme, like the person who thinks of numerous creative opportunities but never follows through or accomplishes any of that which is envisioned.

The fifth chakra is governed by the fifth ray, which has a blue/fuchsia colour, which "gives creativity to life." Fifth ray individuals are our artists, musicians, dancers, as well as actors and actresses. The gift is the gift of unlimited creative and communicative potential.

The shapes in our drawing where Blue is most prominent can reflect that your Throat vortex is activated through the sense of taste.
Take a deep breath and bring in feelings of freedom from the known with the sound of O as in boat. This stimulates our Throat chakra and activates our ability to communicate with our fellow man.
Colour in your energy, and as you are doing so feel ideas of wisdom pouring from you. Imagine that all the blockages that are stuck in the three lower chakras are healed during this exercise.

The gift of this chakra is 'the breath of life.'
Communication is a gift that everyone should have.

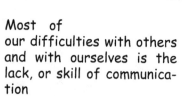

Salute to the Sun
With the sound of a as in say

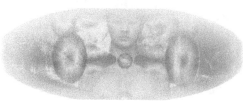

Most of our difficulties with others and with ourselves is the lack, or skill of communication

Look at your energy field and draw away any blocked particles on the next page.

The Fifth pathway for your soul

The Fifth energy channel that energises the physical body through the blue/fuchsia ray

This vortex is centred at the energy of the thyroid gland and it's the portal to our mental conceptual area. There are various ways in which we can active this chakra This we do through sound. The best way is through learning to created harmonic overtones. This technique is quite astonishing. I recommend anyone to attend a singing course or choir, or to find a teacher who can teach you to sing harmonic overtones.

People who are good at karate also use the throat chakra in order to access more energy that they then direct at an object. That is how they, by the power of sound, can break phenomenally thick pieces of wood or even bricks.

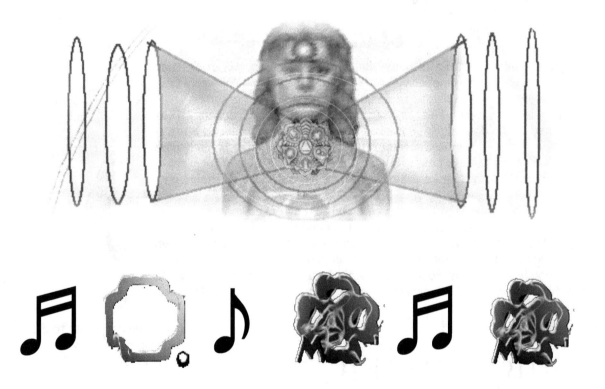

The Sound of Your name

The vibration of your first spoken name at birth is the first sound-melody that you heard from the person that took care of you from the start of this lifetime. In the following exercise we are going to interpret what qualities, talents and characteristics this vibration inspired you on a subconscious level to embody your type of body temple.

Memories from our childhood create energy wavelengths which our mind has stored in our unconscious. Divine feelings of unconditional love is the birthright for everyone, even if one did not receive it through this incarnation.

It's that loving, inspiring, powerful, all inclusive feeling quality that we need to embody in order to wake up from this dream. It is food for the soul. This energy food we call the Language of Light.

Your first used name

The decoding method is done through the numeral vibration that came from your <u>nick name</u>, or your first <u>used name</u>. Those numeral frequencies help us to translate their qualities, gifts and attributes.

Each letter in your first spoken name was a tonal frequency that combined formed a melody. For most of us this melody or sound was enriched with feelings of endearment. Not everyone received a nickname and some people have not experienced this unconditional love from their caretakers, they must take their first name that appears on their birth certificate.

This is the only decoding exercise that I have used in my classes. Annelies has used many different ways to decode our original blueprint.

On the next page you will find two tables where you can do your own decoding of your nickname or first used name before the age of seven.

If you have more than one nickname that was used during that period, only take the one that triggered the most favourable memories for you.

1	2	3	4	5	6	7	8	9
A	B	C	D	E	F	G	H	I
J	K	L	M	N	O	P	Q	R
S	T	U	V	W	X	Y	Z	

Use this number scale to discover the numeral vibes of your name(s)

The Fifth Stage / the Fifth level 125

The first Melody you heard

- Our **Root** number taken from the vowels of our name point to our emotional intelligence.
- The combined numeral vibration of the letters of our name belong to our Physical body type.
- Our **Root** number from the Consonants in our name point to our cognitive intelligence
- You can end up with only key numbers, add them and you can get a root number.
- You will find the number chart in the interpretation section on page199

Vowels

Write your name in the center row......................

Consonants

.... Add your vowels up to their **key / root** number

.... Add your letters to your **key / root** number

.... Add your consonants up to their **root / key** number

Vowels

Write your name in the center row......................

Consonants

.... Add your vowels up to their **key / root** number

.... Add your letters to your **key / root** number

.... Add your consonants up to their **root / key** number

Example Ingrid's nickname was and still is **Kitty**
Ingrid's leader aspect vibration of her nick name **Kitty** has the root number 9.
Ingrid started her life with 6 Language of Light Qualities she needs to embrace with gratitude. These are her souls aspects earned before incarnating into this life.

9 + 7= 16 / 7
K i t t y   5
2 + 2+2 =   6
Total........... 18 / 9

At the back of the workbook you find the interpretation of her example. This will help you to interpret which qualities you were born with. Which Language of Light Qualities have you embodied in the mean time and which vibration could you still embody in order to make this lifetime your last!
No one can know another soul. Five children who have the same parents and get the same love and attention do not grow up with the same opportunities.

The Sound of your Name

The melody of your first name has an energy that accompanied you during the first two to three months of your life. After that time your neuron pathways in your brain were already accumulating many experiences that you stored away. (See figure.....)

The melody your caretakers nurtured you with would always stay a healing vibration but gradually the more and more programmed impressions you accumulated, the more you would feel separated from these loving vibrations.

- First of all colour in the circles with the appropriate colours of the chakras
- Take the key and root numbers from your decoding of your first name and write them next to the writing that explains what the numeral vibrations mean to us in words.
- Your Key numbers must be added to get a root number if the key number is above 48. Look up under which chakra vortex that Key number falls under in your workbook.
- Every chakra has between 5 to 10 language of Light tonal vibrations on the <u>first and second</u> level of Annelies' ascension workshop.
- In total you have to embody at least 48 Language of Light vibrations in order to <u>awaken</u> to a higher consciousness level.
- In Annelies' journal she writes about this third level of awareness.
- The 12 Language of Light Qualities you have already embodied by the time you have done the work in this workbook will prepare you for the ascension process.
- You will start to recognize in others what qualities they have, even without being aware of them.
- Remember, whatever you see in another, you only recognise because it must be embedded in your own energy field.

The 9 consciousness levels	Their colour vibrations	Our I am of Spirit (Full consciousness)
9	○	Our I am of Spirit (Full consciousness)
8	○	Our Oversoul (Cosmic Consciousness)
7	○	Soul aware (Multidimensional awareness)
6	○	Initiation (Becoming aware)
5	○	Self Knowledge (Speaking one's truth)
4	○	Compassion (Unconditional love)
3	○	Self consciousness (Power issues)
2	○	Beliefs (Addictive issues)
1	○	Physical survival (Security issues)

The Fifth Level / the Fifth Stage 127

The Melody at your Birth

My own numeral vibrations	The vibration within the name are the sounds that reflect the qualities and characteristics written below. Study the individual Language of Light Quality of that vibration.
....	**9** Our spirit will be free of attachment to our material form through a dimensional /density shift we call ascension.
....	**8** The actual re-activation of our light body takes place when our over-soul has entered the in-breath. The soul purpose is to return home.
....	**7** Through the reprogramming of our DNA, the body will undergo restructuring to counteract environmental changes. Our physical bodies are ascension temples for the soul.
....	**6** Physical ascension is embraced as an intent. Our light body is activated which increases in vibration. We know what has our passion.
....	**5** One must understand and integrate one's shadow side and acknowledge that all is neither good nor bad, it simply IS. love thyself in others.
....	**4** One acknowledges in everyone the god/goddess within, this will open the heart chakra. Look at the good in others first.
....	**3** One can move beyond karma through learning to love and forgive oneself and others
....	**2** One is responsible for ones own spiritual progress, beliefs are all restricted by dogma.
....	**1** All material things are part of God. Until judgement, denial and guilt are understood, everything we think, say, do or believe keeps us separated from our source.

The 6th Language of Light Quality
Is the symbol of Unconditional Love

The sixth chakra represents the centre where we learn to observe ourselves. This is the centre where our mind can travel into our inner world of bliss, joy and develop an ability to 'see' all things clearly with an intuitive knowledge. The law of cause and effect are recognised and we can see the subtle laws that govern man on the psychic and spiritual levels. When this chakra is fully active a spiritually discerning person can look clairvoyantly into their Akashic records, or sometimes into others.

This is the chakra that 'when damaged' people feel threatened by any unseen phenomenon. Any psychic phenomenon is taboo when the personality is strongly represented by the Sacral Chakra. The need for sensational escapes in order to deal with emotional stresses can become addictions and the sixth chakra closes off. These people are their own worst enemy but through emotional pain they will trigger their 'wake-up call'.

Guidelines

During this mind-drawing exercise again we address the 'body avatar' to assist us in this exercise.

- You now know with which Language of Light Quality you came into this world.
- How does this knowing help you to assess your awareness at this moment?
- What came up for you when you did your honour yourself mandala drawing?
- Close your eyes for a moment and look within. Imagine this vortex spinning into the unlimited universe.
- See what your symbol of unconditional love looks like.

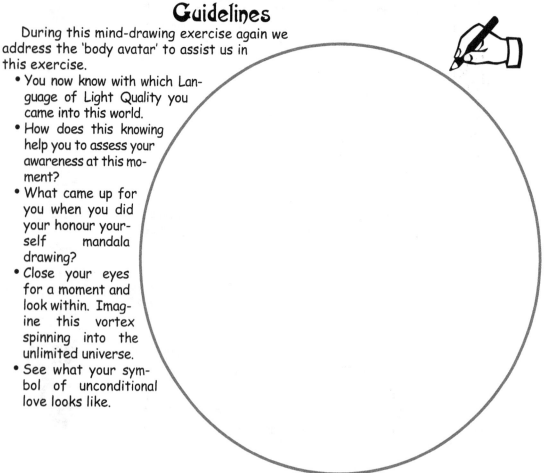

Your Language of Light Card of <u>Unconditional Love</u>

Again draw your final 6th symbol of Unconditional love within your Language of Light card. This gift feels like a love affair of the heart.

Tip

When you have finished, have two colour copies made of your 6th Language of Light card, reduce it to a business card size. Paste one in your Language of Light card at the back of the workbook in the booklet section. And laminate the other

The Third Eye Chakra: your Higher mind channel

With the symbol of Unconditional Love

This sixth chakra which is associated with our inner wisdom rather than expressing outward into the world. This vortex sits directly behind the centre of the eyebrows and is connected to the pituitary gland, which is intimately connected to the pineal gland. Our pineal is involved in the perception of light particles called photons.

- This **6**th frequency of Unconditional love when embodied, then we experience a true love affair of the heart. The 2nd and 11th frequency of Structure and Direction from the Sacral Chakra are of a similar tonal vibration.
- The **15**th frequency of Prosperity is embodied in people who are generous without any fear of ever having less than others.
- The frequency that the **24**th frequency stimulates in our physical experience is to comprehend Oneness with everything. This 'knowing' will open our psychic Third Eye in order to see visions from the causal plane. The quality of integrity (29) must be practised.

- This **33**rd master frequency when embodied will help us to see through the illusion of the 3rd dimension. When we experience communion (38) with all of nature, we gradually experience that our physical life is the 'dream' while our dream state takes us temporarely into the world where we came from.
- The frequency that the **42**nd octave brings is the gift of true Communication. When we have embraced the art of listening, we have embodied the frequency of Humanhood **(47)** and Telepathy, Clairvoyance and Psychometry consciousness is added to our daily awareness.

The Fifth Level / the Fifth Stage 131

Your Third Eye Chakra Card

When your draw yet again your conscious awareness symbol remember that the card ends up being very small. Your artwork is greatly reduced. Now that you know some other Language of Light qualities you can add them in your chakra card.

Tip

When you have finished, have two colour copies made of your Third Eye Chakra card, reduce it to a business card size. Paste one at the back of the workbook in the booklet section. And laminate the other

Your Mandala is a reflection of your real self

Do we live to our full potential?

What is our full potential? POWAH repeatedly states that we are gods in the making. We are already masters at a great many things. He said that we have to drop the idea of becoming someone, because we already are a masterpiece. We cannot be improved, we have only to come to it, to know it, to realize it.

A mandala is a magic circle. Symbolic systems like the science of chakras, the kabbalah, numerology and astrology all stem from the base structure of a mandala format. Through the Mandala on the next page we are going to express on paper how to live out our full potential, or how to break through the programme of our personality 'body type' in an Analogue Symbolism way.

Through the following exercise we are both the artist (personality) and the observer (higher self) As we watch our thoughts being transferred into images, those images are imbued with energy (beams of light) because we can see them with our inner Third Eye. Our physical eye is the human intermediary between the gift of outer light,(what we see physically) and the beams of light we see in our imagination.

Drawing our own mandala through the five stages we have been working with in the following exercise creates a window into our creative inner universe. We will travel into multidimensional territories (unconsciousness mind) so that our thoughts and ideas become visible and known to our conscious mind.

Understanding the primordial symbolism of the mandala can lead to greater awareness. We also learn to make a shift in our approach to our two dimensional linear left thinking mode towards our spatial right thinking mode. Through this mandala design once again we probe the language of our psyche in order to reveal your personal symbolic language. We call this the LANGUAGE OF YOUR LIGHT.

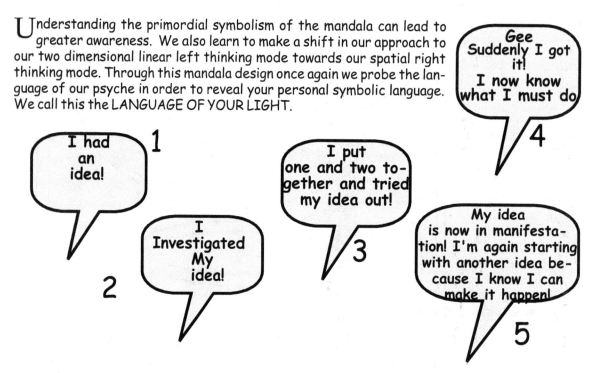

The Magic Circle Within

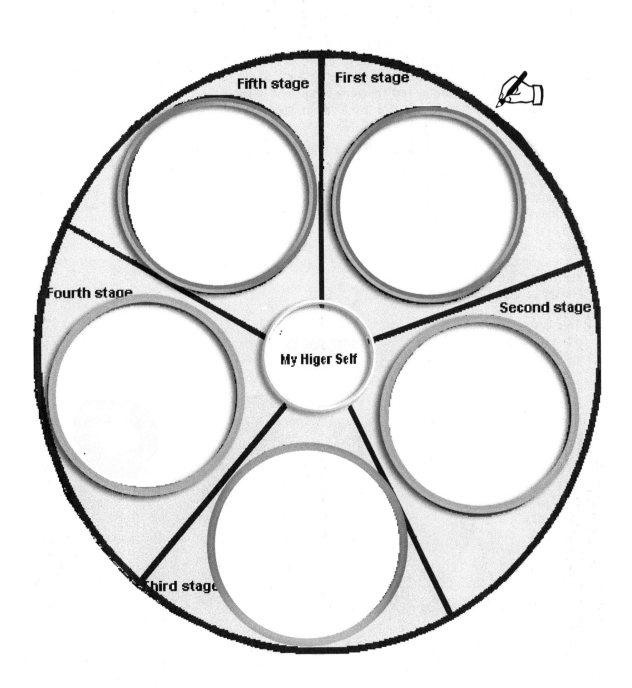

Your 7th Language of Light Quality
Is the symbol of Freedom

The Seventh chakra gives us an awareness of karma. When we work with this chakra we will intuitively know that all the hardships or obstacles in our lives were chosen before we even incarnated. This is hard to accept, but many people know that from deep within, they are starting to see how they attracted the very conditions in their lives. Blaming tendencies that were personality based reactions are gradually replaced by moving with an observing mode.

Guidelines

- When we start to become aware that nothing in our lives is meaningless, even the bad times, our lives will become enriched with new opportunities. When we embody the first 10 to 48 qualities of the Language of Light, our lives will be so full of joy, happiness, adventure and bliss, we wondered how we ever survived without our Higher selves Love energy.
- This is your Language Of Light quality that will open the channel for all the other Qualities to come in.
- This quality gift of freedom will lift the veil from our eyes.
- Take a deep breath and bring in feelings of joy and peace from the sound of U as in sun This will stimulate our Crown Chakra and activate our ability to be in the moment.

Your Language of Light Card of Freedom

Draw your Language of light symbol of Freedom in the circle within your card. With this 7th frequency the soul carries the gift of freedom into the new paradigm.

Tip

When you have finished, have two colour copies made of your 7th Language of Light card, reduce it to a business card size. Paste one in your Language of Light card at the back of the workbook in the booklet section. And laminate the other

The vibration of your Third Eye energy field

The sixth channel that energises the physical body through the Violet/indigo ray

This awakened awareness will create an abundance of opportunities in our lives. It is also connected with our Sacral Chakra, which is where our personalities dwell. On this level our higher self will mostly be in control of our lives. This Violet and Orange ray, when blended in perfect balance, creates a golden colour within our auric field.

This love vibration is based on **freedom**, independence and the urge to serve.

A daily acknowledgement with gratitude for another day will draw more of our soul-force into our physical lives and reveal truths that have before been hidden(20).

When we draw out the energy field on this level, we must be aware that our analogue drawings are a reflection of our state of mind at that moment. When we express and draw our conflicts, worries, dreams, hurts, fears and joys and our real inner feelings out on paper, we are looking at our mirror.

When we draw out our inspirations, our dreams, or our love for others, then this energy helps us to truly give from the heart without needing to receive.

Sixth ray individuals are our visionaries, clairvoyants, and healers. The gift inherent within the sixth ray is the gift of seeing all things, including one's dark side.

As you draw this energy field, think of travelling.

This can mean travelling on our inner planes, during our dream time, or going on a holiday.

What does the word Freedom mean to you?

The Sixth pathway of your soul

The sixth channel that energises the physical body through the Violet/indigo ray

Take a deep breath and bring in feelings of joy and peace. This will activate our ability to be in this world but not of it.
Colour in your energy, and as you are doing so feel the word of wisdom pouring from you. Imagine that all the blockages that are stuck in the three lower chakras are healed during this exercise.

As we grow into higher consciousness, we increasingly realize that we are not just the bodies we live in. Our physical bodies are our soul's vehicle of consciousness. Before any incarnation the soul chooses a genetic lineage that will manifest certain experiences. Through the decoding of our genetic blueprint with Annelies, I learned what the difference was between our soul lineage and our genetic ancestral heritage.

Our parents, brothers and sisters do not necessarily belong to our soul lineage but a close friend might.

Why do we choose the parents we did, who is a soul mate and who is not? What do people call a twin soul?

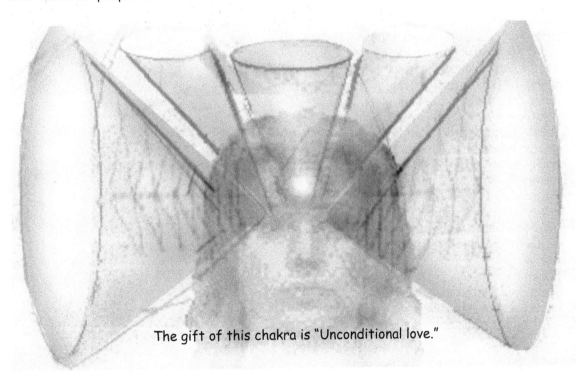

The gift of this chakra is "Unconditional love."

138 The Language of Light

The Crown Chakra: your cosmic awareness mind

With the symbol of Freedom

No words in any language, apart from the Language of Light, can really describe what feelings this centre gives to our daily lives, because it is the highest spiritual energy that is seen in colours like violet that is blending with red and blue in perfect balance.

- The **7**th Language of Light frequency brings us the wonderful gift of the energy of freedom. This energy gives our spirit the motivation to live for our soul purpose.
- The **9**th Language of Light vibration, the frequency of unity brings a feeling of belonging.
- The **16**th numeral tone awakens a consciousness awareness of magnitude. This gift helps us to recognize the value in every experience.
- With the **8**th frequency of the quality the word function reflects, our higher self is able to be of service to humanity in our physical consciousness plane
- The **25**th gift in the 'inner knowing', we often call truth, is perceived by every one differently, but in the end we will experience that all is one.
- The **27**th vibration that creates a fluidity in our lives has the gift of 'time' by keeping us in the moment. Only then can we perceive of a world where 'time' is no more, it's just an illusion.
- The quality of the **34**th Language of Light frequency gives us passion for our awakening.
- The powerful **36**th Language of Light frequency that we experience as sexual energy brings us the closest to perceive creation in action.
- The wavelength that the **43**rd Language of Light quality brings to us is the ability to perceive the elemental world of the nature kingdom. For many people this is still an unknown world.
- The last **45**th Language of Light frequency is the one we need to embody in order to go on the ascension journey. This is a plane where souls receive their records of all the incarnations they accumulated.

Your Crown Chakra Card

Take your time when you create this etheric chakra. This centre is only in action when the six vortexes below are vibrating in harmony. People who have moments of a taste of this centre use words like; blissful state of peace, heaven, nirvana.

Tip

When you have finished, have two colour copies made of your Crown Chakra card, reduce it to a business card size. Paste one in your Base card at the back of the workbook in the booklet section. And laminate the other

Crown Chakra

The vibration level of your Etheric energy field

The Seventh channel that energises the etheric body through the Magenta ray

We have reached the seventh energy vortex, which is an etheric chakra. That means this vortex exists within the realm of the psyche; it is our channel to our Higher Self, which has an expanded awareness. It lies at the crown of the head, corresponding to the Pineal gland, which to me feels like the anchoring point of the human soul.

This centre is our gateway to cosmic intelligence. It only resonates with the highest purpose of our human existence. It has the potential of assessing full awareness.

People who have moments of a taste of this centre use words like; blissful state of peace, heaven, nirvana. It's the quality of inner silence where we visit in our dream time. This is the realm where any emotional energies we experienced during an incarnation are replayed back to us if necessary.

- Colour in your energy, and as you are doing so feel the words of love pouring from your higher self into the top of your head. Imagine that all the blockages that are stuck in all the six lower chakras are healed during this exercise.
- When this chakra is fully active the ageing process has stopped. In many people this starts to happen when they already have reached an age where others would think of retiring and slowing down.
- Instead these people have new tasks that keeps them busy.
- They make sure that every day counts.
- An enlightened man cannot be enslaved and he cannot be imprisoned.
- That is the gift of Cosmic Awareness.

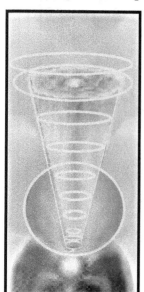

Salute to the Sun With the sound of O as in Home

The Seventh pathway of your soul

The Seventh channel that energises the etheric body through the Magenta ray

As we grow into higher consciousness, we increasingly realize that we are much more than the personality, and that our higher self can become a channel for our soul force to enter so that our spiritual life force, that is eternal, can rejuvenate all the cells of our bodies.

Only if we break through the cage of our conditioning and reach the truth of our own hearts can we begin to see life as it really is.

We are entering the dawn of a new understanding. Veils into other worlds have never been closed to us, they have always been there for us to explore.

As you visualise the energy field of your crown chakra with all its worlds within worlds, allow your higher self to be a travelling guide.

Our Psychic vision centre

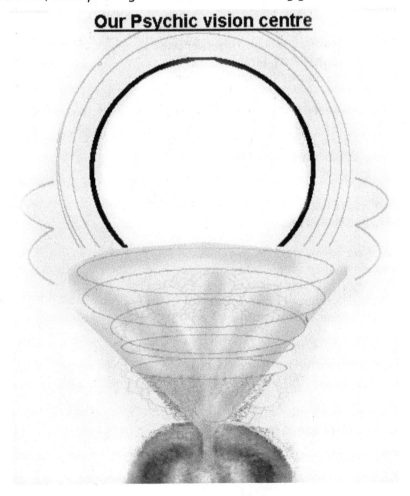

The Auric field of your Soul body

Through the colouring energies I discovered the Real Me

We live in special times. We hear that a lot these days but why would our time be more special? What is time anyway. This dream we call reality, if it is just a fragment or a facet that is stored in our akashic records like a movie script. Could we not step out of this movie and look back at our movie as if we are in a movie theatre? Then we become our own observer!

It's that simple. POWAH said that it's all in the intent of each individual person what they have chosen to accomplish during this incarnation. When we have at least eliminated about 50% of our addictive programming, our Over Soul will know if our individual soul came into this incarnation in order to physically ascend; meaning reaching full consciousness.

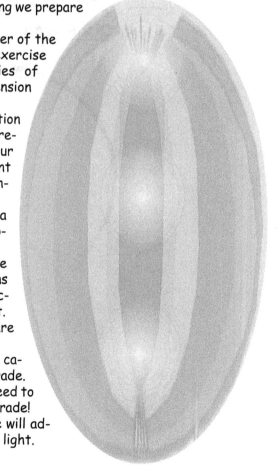

We have come to the end of our awakening journey through the chakra's. During this last mind-drawing we prepare ourselves for our Light Body work.

You have by now become familiar with the power of the Language of our spiritual light. Through this exercise we will consciously embody at least ten qualities of our Language of Light frequencies on our ascension journey.

Annelies calls our awakening also a resurrection period. When we increase our vibratory frequency of our physical body sufficiently, our body's cellular structure is sped up to the point of becoming invisible to ordinary third dimensional consciousness.

Your Language of Light symbols will act like a clearing device for the release of addictive programming.

The feelings that we have attached to these symbols will pulsate their healing vibrations throughout your energy field. This will in turn activate the DNA strands that have been dormant.

We have even more than 12 strands that are not in use!

Humanity has been using a limited memory capacity. Our biological computer needs an upgrade. We need more memory space! This means we need to use more energy in order to qualify for an upgrade!

It's far more complicated than that but we will address this during the activation of our body of light.

The Fifth Level / the Fifth Stage 143

How consciously Aware is your soul in this incarnation? Let's give our soul an age on an awareness scale. This means that for our soul to be fully aware through the human body it must partake more of it's divine energy.

- This **5th** stage is difficult to attain. Achieving it usually requires a detached life style and a long period of intense consciousness growth practice to fully awaken the soul.

- During the **4th** stage in our lives our soul, through our Higher self, becomes actively involved.

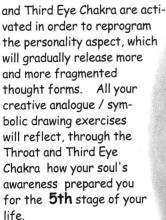

Both the Throat and Third Eye Chakra are activated in order to reprogram the personality aspect, which will gradually release more and more fragmented thought forms. All your creative analogue / symbolic drawing exercises will reflect, through the Throat and Third Eye Chakra how your soul's awareness prepared you for the **5th** stage of your life.

- During the **3rd** stage in our lives our personality addictions must be released, to make room for our emotional intelligence from the Higher self. Only when our Heart Chakra is active can our Higher Self act as a channel for our soul.
- When people forgive themselves for their own created hardships, disappointments and disillusions, many people awaken to their soul purpose and start to follow their heart's desires. They learned over the years how joy, peace and harmony is necessary in order to be of service to themselves and their fellow man. All your creative analogue/symbolic drawing exercises will reflect, through the Heart chakra how your soul's awareness prepared you for the **4th** stage of your life.

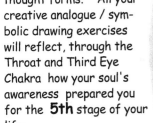

During the **1st** stage of our lives our soul must be motivated to become aware through the physical form. During our growing up stage, say between the age of 0---7---14---21 you experienced early childhood, school years, highschool, college or university. All your creative analogue/symbolic drawing exercises will reflect, through the Base Chakra, how your souls embodied awareness prepared you for the **2nd** stage of your life.

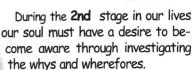

During the **2nd** stage in our lives our soul must have a desire to become aware through investigating the whys and wherefores.

- This questioning starts at different age levels in different people. Many children that are born today already are very aware and they start investigating during their early school years. Some people only start questioning during their late twenties, early thirties or during the forties. Some never do. Your creative analogue/symbolic drawing exercises will reflect, through the Sacral and the Solar Plexus Chakra how your soul's awareness prepared you for the **3rd** stage of your life.

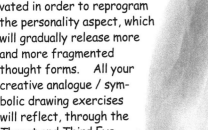

144 The Language of Light

The Language of Light Symbols of 8th <u>Divine union</u> and 9th <u>Unity</u> are added to your Auric field. (Use the cards at the back of the workbook.)

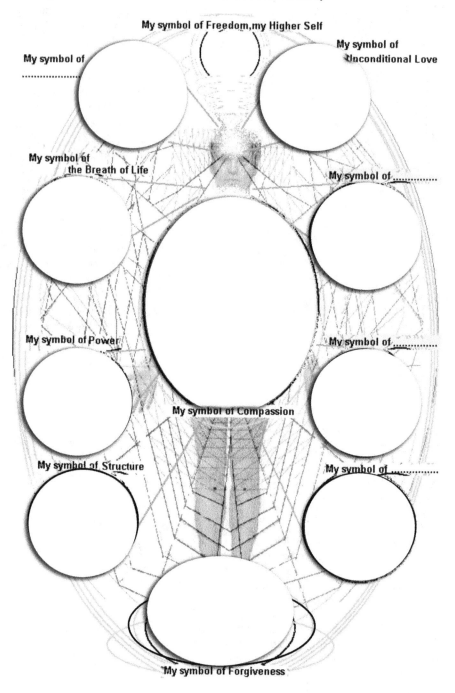

The Language of Light Symbols of 8th <u>Divine union</u> and 9th <u>Unity</u> are added to your Auric field. (Use the cards at the back of the workbook.)

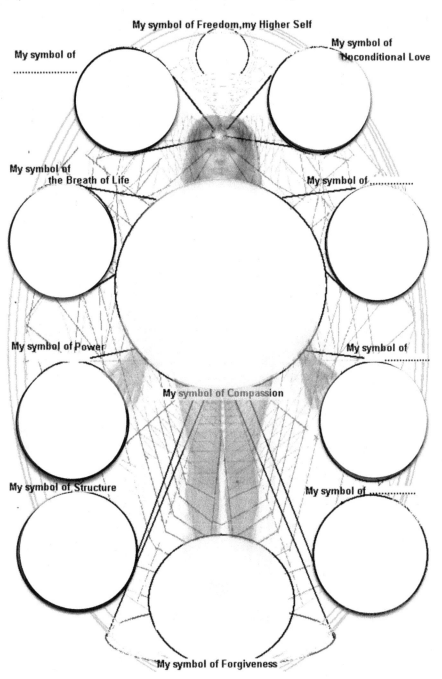

Your Fifth insight

On the Fifth Creative Stage Surrounding your Idea.

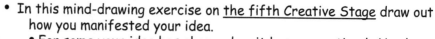

- In this mind-drawing exercise on <u>the fifth Creative Stage</u> draw out how you manifested your idea.
  - For some your <u>idea</u> has changed or it has concretized. You have taken action and have started to manifest the results.
  - If your idea was a long term one you will soon reap the benefits of your intent.
  - Whatever you do, do it joyfully. Do it for the good of all.
  - When your whole life becomes creative, you will bring great joy into the world.
- On a spiritual level you are ready to activate your body of light.

Your Fifth insight

Make notes on this page about what you have learned during this fifth stage. On this stage you have experienced what it is like to have control over your manifestations. Write down what has come up for you during this fifth stage.

On a soul level this stage is not easy to reach, but many will start to get glimpses of what the fifth stage is all about.

We have no more attachments to mundane needs and expectations. We have learned to go with the flow and at the same time sidestep the obstacles we experiences before. We are fully aware of the 'reality' dream.

Write down your thoughts on the whole five stages experience. What insights were the most profound.

....
....
....
....
....
....
....
....
....
....
....
....
....
....
....

Activation Of Your Body of Light

Our Light Body

Anyone who has the desire to awaken to full consciousness has to create a vehicle, or a temple through which their consciousness can travel inter-dimensionally into higher realms of existence. For many this is experienced as an inner journey.

Through our Light body we create or relive different realities that are all taken from our akashic records. We explore the records of our unconscious with the help of the elemental, mineral and angelic kingdoms.

Evolution of the human species

Let's contemplate that millions of years ago, our ancestors never perceived the world the way we do today. They perceived energy as energy, not like we perceive energy. We know that everything is energy but we perceive that our world is made up of concrete objects.

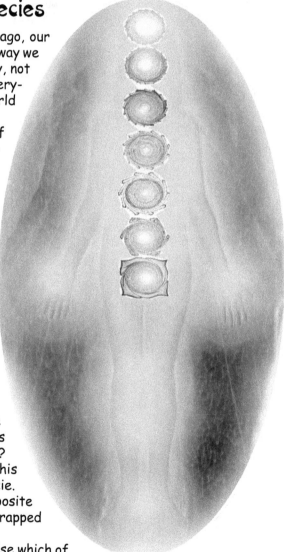

Let's look at evolution from a soul's point of view. Let's assume that our soul, that embodied the first human root race, had a completely different body to experience 'life' as we know it today. This body or vehicle was more like a light body. Why? Let's say that this 'light body was created by a Magnetic energy force. When we dropped our soul consciousness into a denser realm, something must have shifted our magnetic vibrational manifestations.

Maybe that's how our concept of 'aliens' came into the picture. Imagine if souls, let's call them the 'Nephilim' that had been embodying creations in other universes and galaxies, became interested in the human creation. Could it be that somehow they merged their Electric force field with our original Magnetic force field and we have gradually become a species that is formed by an Electro-Magnetic energy force?

Topics on Alien species is not part of this workbook so we will stick to the Human specie.

It seems that when the world of two opposite polarities came into existence, we became trapped into the dream of our own making.

Throughout this workbook you will recognise which of the five energy expressions influences you the most.

We are all Energy Beings.

Annelies has influenced my idea that there are five types of energies. I have called those energies; Magnetic, Electric, Radio-active, Magneto-electric and Electro-Magnetic waves of frequencies. If we hold on to the idea that all our thoughts, which are clusters of energies, fall under any of

- I say it is through the <u>physical body</u> that we have to experience transformation, not just in <u>our minds</u>.
- Our <u>higher self</u>, which is our observer, is the part of us that perceives the world as pure energy.
- It's the <u>lower self,</u> our persona or EGO, (with the help of inorganic entities) that seem to be in control of our lives most of the time. Through that conscious awareness level we see the world as a 'reality' where everything is solid.

We are also influenced by:

- Electric—Male energy.
- Magnetic—Female energy.
- And Radio-active—distorted energy.

The idea is to move into balance. Let's assume that our physical human body was originally manifested as an Electromagnetic energy bubble. Annelies calls that our blueprint. I speculate that the fall of consciousness might have to do with the other four energy expressions that corrupted our creation. It seems to make sense that our 'fall in consciousness' ultimately teaches us how to be co-creators.

By now most of us know that the planet is undergoing a shift towards a higher frequency. Our whole solar system is moving and shifting. Because our planet is a living ascending energy system, all who reside within her energy field will also experience this realignment.

Annelies allowed me to read a section of her journal(novel) named:

The Return of the Initiate.

I read in her journal that our physical bodies are changing from a carbon based body to a crystalline body. Meaning we emit more light into our cells, we will become less dense in physical matter. Our so-called junk DNA, is activated.

What could or does this all mean?

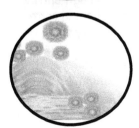

Our Ascension into a new Paradigm

People who follow spirit or 'who have a desire to become aware' all have one thing in common. They are increasing their ability to feel more Heart centered compassion.

This can only be attained by choosing new behaviours and to integrate or release our fear-based characteristics. As we gradually change the frequency of our bodies, we will experience physical changes.

Visualise your body like a balloon. As you start to perceive more or become more aware, you are filling your body with helium (light). The more helium you have in a balloon, the higher it rises. The more compassion (light) we can hold in our bodies through emotional clearing, we spin towards the light. Our consciousness increases, and our dormant DNA strands will be activated. Due to you stating an <u>intent</u> to become aware, or awake, the soul will embody more energy and learns to adapt to the physical changes in order to support the increase in vibration.

By Heart centred compassion. I don't mean head centred or intellectual compassion. There is a difference.

Doing a lot of charity work because you feel sorry for others is a waste of time.

If you are truly drawn to be surrounded with people who are either starving or have aids, to mention a few energy distortions, that is different so long as you feel an inner joy while doing it. Your work MUST have your passion!

Nobody is anywhere where they should not be, even children who get maimed during a war have an important role to play in the scheme of things. We all emotionally react when we are confronted with sadness, pain and loss of life. We all want to save the world, but there is nothing to save. It's all a dream; a nightmare for some.

How do we know why some souls choose to experience a lot of sorrow, pain or hardships in the dream?

Annelies warned us that the ascension path takes a heavy toll on our emotional, mental and physical bodies, since it necessitates the purging and balancing of both upper and lower chakras.

Through uniting oneself with the infinite Source of our Spirit life; establishing contact with our Higher Self; giving respect to all life; deliberately finding beauty <u>everywhere</u>; clearing our sense of perceptions; as well as establishing and working within a body of light, we can create a new 'reality'. This will set us free in order to fully enter into the new paradigm.

Lets journey outside the limits of our reasoning.
Into the inner world of the dreamer.

Most people will argue that nothing can be outside the limits of reason; things can be obscure, but sooner or later reason always finds a way to shed light on anything. Annelies taught me that 'reason' is only a by-product of our habitual (programmed) perception. The more rigid and stationary it is, the greater our confidence in ourselves. In the old paradigm that worked. All the success books and positive thinking books used that media for gain and also in order to empower the personas of the human race! The time has arrived when even positive thinking philosophy does not work any more!

The greater our feeling of <u>knowing</u> the world we live in, the greater our power to be able to predict the outcome, but we need all our divine energy to do so!

For thousands of years only through our dreams, meditations and visions could we enter into other worlds and perceive the inconceivable.

What is the inconceivable?

A world where there is no war, no starvation, no illness, NO DEATH.

If we all embrace that possibility, we have moved into a new paradigm where we as human beings can again journey back to the stars and become the co-creators we always were.

Through the mind-drawings you will become more and more aware of how your perceptions can make a shift. During these exercises we journey through unthinkable dimensions that make us perceive the previously inconceivable, the intelligence of your physical body.

Our body responds to our environment and to our thoughts and the feeling we have about our body. Our bodies respond to the way we treat them in terms of hygiene, food intake, rest and exercise.

When we entered this incarnation, the language of our physical body was wired in at birth and formed the foundation for our soul memories.

Through our mind-drawing, when we start to really listen to our physical body, we can learn a great deal about the qualities and the characteristics of our soul.

You will see that many of the symbols of the Language of Light used in the ascension board game, are reflected by the drawings below. They all describe the different moods in colour, shape and line in a symbolic way. Your personal Language of Light symbols will also create an energy link to the language of your physical body. Why? Because your physical body is the biological consciousness of your soul!

Elemental Alchemy

Through the second half of this mind-drawing workbook you will journey with me through the elements of
- <u>Fire, Earth, Water, Air and Ether.</u>
- Those are the elements that respond to our daily thought. The additional element of wood and metal brings to our attention how we gradually lost our soul awareness.

ETHER

- During the activation of the Body of Light we will call special attention to the much-overlooked element of ether. Ether is a medium that permeates all space and transmits waves of energy in a wide range of frequencies, from cell phones to human auras. What is "ethereal" is related to the regions beyond earth: the heavens.
- Ether as an element is lacking in material substance, but is no less real than wood, stone or flesh. POWAH said that; "Within the context of ether there can be a fusion of the polarities."

We are moving into a new paradigm and gradually our 3rd dimensional realm will move into the 5th dimensional realm. We will move from one dream over to another. That is why the element of ether plays a big role. This light energy manifests no more darkness or light in people, but instead creates an uplifted fusion. We need to put our entire mind and heart into pursuing unity and fusion with the element of ether. 'Inorganic beings' (our lower persona) cannot enter this 5th realm.

Through your mind-drawing exercises you will experience how the different colour rays of light with the harmonic overtones of sound can express symbols that relate to the platonic shapes. These shapes are the building blocks of our physical creation.

This creative inner journey will also trigger and release dysfunctional blocked energies.

As always, use discernment when viewing your drawings. Accept only the message that feels right in your heart.

When you are in a group, only observe each other's higher Self during the whole mind-drawing procedure. Become aware that your ego is like our shadow, it follows us around, but when the light is shining from above, it merges with our highest intent!

Colour, Shape and our Senses

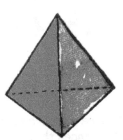
Tetrahedron

Our world is composed of 5 basic elements, each represented by a particular shape, characteristic and quality. These elements are linked to a colour and they influence our first symbolic expressions of our physical experiences. These elements are called platonic solids. They form a special version of the science of Geometry.

Octahedron

These elements also form the blueprint for all the cell structures in the physical bodies of humans, animals plants and minerals.

Before you took on this new incarnation, your soul chose a body type that would serve it best in this life time.

Your body type influences your personality and characteristics of this incarnation. The Platonic Solids we have used as formats in our mind-drawings are special versions of Sacred Geometry.

The shapes based on triangles traditionally represent **male** energy.

The **Hexahedron**, (the square) represents **female** energy.

Hexahedron

This 6x4 solid is associated with the element of <u>Earth</u>, the mammal, our sense of smell and the colour green.

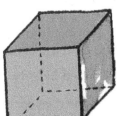
Hexahedron

Dodecahedron

This 12x5 solid, representing the pentagon format and the facets are associated with <u>Ether</u>, spirit, touch, and the colour violet.

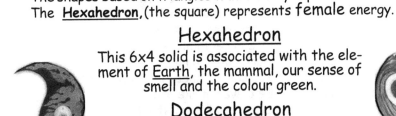

Male   Female

Icosahedron

This 20x3 solid is associated with <u>Water</u>, the reptile, taste, and the colour blue.

Icosahedron

Tetrahedron

This 4x3 solid is associated with <u>Fire</u>, man, sight, recognition, consciousness, and the colour red.

Octahedron

This 8x3 solid is associated with <u>Air</u>, the bird, sound and the colour yellow.

Dodecahedron

The 48 Universal Language of Light symbols
That will activate your DNA/RNA

Once a soul reaches the fourth level of awareness, many begin to consciously draw in experiences that maximize their growth. The soul often attracts a lesson that the ego fights, resists or complains about instead of accepting the lesson as a gift.
Now that you have gone through the activations of the chakras by embodying quite a few qualities of the 48 Language of Light attributes, the following mind-drawing work can prepare you for the activation of your light body.

The first 48 Language of Light quality symbols take you into a fourth density realm otherwise called the new paradigm. This realm is vibrating on a far higher level than the third density realm.

Some very evolved souls have chosen to re-experience third density situations in order to gain valuable experiences not available in the higher realms, so don't ever think I'm implying that third density humans are any less divine than higher vibrating beings.

In order to know on which level you mostly operate you simply look at some of the programming that is still actively applied.

The Third Density Assessments are.

- Without an earthly body I cannot live..........
- I ought to get all I can...............................
- Matter is everything....................................
- All life is uncertain.....................................
- Place faith in nothing..................................
- You cannot make life pay without cheating..
- Make others think you are clever.................
- Satisfy your desires....................................
- Overcome good with evil.............................
- Create chaos, then control what you will.....
- Make others accept your discipline.............
- Revenge all wrongs....................................
- Is it worthwhile making efforts to help anyone?
- Life is here for me to experience................

The Fourth density Assessments are

- I cannot live on Earth without a body
- I can get all I ought
- Everything matters
- Life is certainly All
- Place faith in no "Thing'
- You cannot cheat Life without paying.
- Be clever, make others think
- Desire to be satisfied.
- Overcome Evil with good
- Control chaos, then create what you will
- Discipline yourself to make others accept you
- Revenge is wrong
- Make efforts to help anyone worthwhile
- I am here to experience Life

As William Gray says:"an action, which means expenditure of energy, is always convertible into other terms." I call them short term and long term assessments

The fifth density body is visible to fourth density humans as a luminescent outline of the physical form. At first such visions will be psychic. When our Third Eye is spinning at the right wavelength, all sorts of entities are discovered within the grid formations of the ethers.

Symbolic Energy Particles 157

The first 48 Language of Light symbol chart from the 7 major chakras
(These symbols are used by the spiritual school of ascension)

7	9	16	18	25	27	34	36	43	45
Freedom	Unity	Magnitude	Function	Truth	Fluidity	Passion	Sexual Energy	Unknown Worlds	Underwater Worlds

Add your own Seven Language of Light Symbols Below And colour Any other LoL Qualities your Name revealed

6	15	24	33	42
Unconditional Love	Prosperity	Oneness	Illusion	Communication

5	14	23	32	41
Breath of Life	Abundance	External expressions	Dreams	Honesty

4	8	13	17	22	26	31	35	40	44
Compassion	Divine union	Peace	Intuition	Instinctive	Action	Honour	Creativity	Hidden worlds	Community

3	12	21	30	39	48
Power	Hope	Consciousness	Balance	Dance of Life	God/Goddess

2	11	20	29	38	47
Structure	Direction	Hidden truth	Integrity	Communion	Humanhood

1	10	19	28	37	46
Forgiveness	Peaceful Bliss	Perseverance	Purpose	Friendship	Global unity

1	2	3	4	5	6	7

How your Kundalini energy travels through the **spinning** chakras.

Our Original Blueprint

The genetic codes of your physical body

RNA and DNA are actual programme codes. When I started to work with computers, I was amazed how technology made me see how our human bio-computer(our brain) works. When when we look at a computer screen showing us a beautiful picture that even moves and has sound we are amazed at our clever inventions. Even our cell phones can project the same images. What makes it work? To most of us the HTML codes, look like gobbledegook, but those are the codes that create a virtual reality effect on our screens!

Imagine that our 'reality' came into existence more or less the same way! Imagine that our Soul, which is the library of our life force (spirit) that holds an indescribable amount of 'codes' creates our physical, emotional, mental, and intuitive, creative bodies, then it is correct to say that we are not our bodies, we are much more than that. So...our bodies are the expression of our soul!

What has this all got to do with our light body? Well, if we are moving into a 5th density realm would you not like to have a body that can experience that realm consciously?

The vibration of the 5th density realm is etheric, meaning the word ETHER is derived from the fact that it is a substance that can disappear into other forms. We already have an invisible double called our etheric body. It's our Etheric body that holds the set of electromagnetic codes that form the programming of our RNA/DNA molecules. The complexities behind the science of ascension are beyond the scope of this workbook. Annelies is far more informed to explain the scientific theories. With the help of others and POWAH they have published articles on the ascension-workshops level 1-2 -3

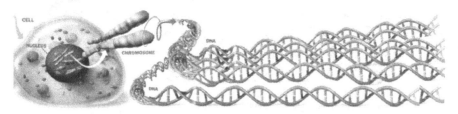

You do not have to be an artist to do mind-drawings, likewise you do not have to study the science of gravity to ride a bike, but.......

You have to be HUMAN.....

to stimulate and activate your RNA/DNA codes.

Your Five Observation points

Seen through the five Elementals

During my studies with Annelies I learned that the awareness of our daily world is so programmed to the smallest detail (although often unnoticed) that it's powerful enough to keep this illusion of 'reality' intact to the minute detail. Annelies said that if we could give that kind of attention to the following five observation points, we will break the illusionary spell we are all under.

The attention I'm referring to is often attained if we have the <u>intent</u> to do so. It's all in the 'intent'. During the following five mind drawing exercises you will create five elemental cards and five more Language of Light cards. Like the seven chakra cards with the seven Language of Light cards, these mind-drawing exercises are like meditations. Your focus and intent will add more psychic energy than you need to awaken to full consciousness.

1 Your Body awareness through the Earth element

A great deal of opportunity will be found by <u>observation and attention to your body</u>. Our physical body must connect with our planetary being. During our first observation point we ask for the assistance from the Earth elemental to ground us.

While you follow the instructions given with each mind-drawing exercise, visualise how your observer <u>sees</u> how cosmic energy filaments travel towards each cell, molecule and atom that make up your body.

This observation alone assembles our reality into a perception. It's our <u>rational mind</u> that instantly arranges what it conceives into a perception of our earthly 3rd dimension.

POWAH explained that it takes a great deal of energy to shift and re-arrange this perception in order to see through the illusion. In order to consciously become aware of other realms we need to have access to more of our cosmic soul energy.

2 Your Body awareness through the Fire element

If our chakras are starting to spin faster due to the fact that we have embodied all the 48 Language of Light Qualities, our awareness is shifting because we have managed to shift our observer's point of view.

We now observe our world from a higher awareness. We are still very much part of this reality and we slip back often, but we start to recognise a difference. Any experience that activates a reaction will trigger our observation point. Because that is uncomfortable, it's our emotional intelligence that makes us slip back to where it was.

It's through the Fire element, our Sacral Sexual chakra and later our Solar Plexus that we learn to maintain more energy.

3 Your Body awareness through the Water element

Through this third observation point our attention is guided by our emotional sensitivity. We start to be very good at reading between the lines so to speak. We can sense our world from a feeling awareness rather than a thinking one. If our Heart chakra is opened our creative /intuitive body is activated. From this observation point some people start to see into the causal plane. Annelies has that ability.

The causal plane is a plane of reality where physical manifestations are test runs up to 2-4 years ahead of time. 70% of people's manifestations are limited through their beliefs. Their thoughts keep creating distortions, which appear as inorganic entities in their dreams. The causal plane unites with the physical plane when a person has stayed focussed on their original intent to ascend.

People who are good tarot readers or use other predictive esoteric practices derive their insights from this causal plane.

Annelies warned us that it can create great karma to the practitioner to tell someone their future. That is because of the belief program that 70% of people still hold on to.

4 Your Body awareness through the Air element

Through the fourth observation point we become dreamers. Richard is a good example. On this awareness level we start to remember our dreams and we know how to direct our dream state. We can retrieve a great deal of information from our akashic records and we can travel to the Astral Plane where our ancestors' consciousness lingers after their existence from their physical incarnations. Genetic related karma is stored on this plane of reality. Astral plane creations are influenced by 30% of dreamers fear-based beliefs; which also often appear as inorganic entities.

If we are more aware on this level our Throat chakra is stimulated by breathing and singing practices. We can now reach our Unconscious and Subconscious Dreamtime Plane. This is a non-physical dream time plane that manifests at the exact opposite to physical plane experiences. No fear-based beliefs apply to that realm. From now on we can explore the start of the fifth density realm.

5 Your Body awareness through the Ether element

We have now completely integrated the causal plane. We start to experience that 'time' can be manipulated. We are very sensitive on a intuitive and psychic level. Mental telepathy becomes a normal communication media. Ingrid and Toon share that ability and so does Annelies and her family. We can shift our observation point at will. The dream and the dreamer flow into one. The ascension process has started. Our Third eye chakra is active and the channel through our etheric crown chakra that links to our higher self is open.

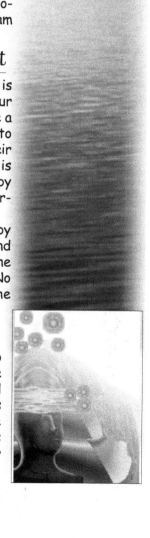

Your Five Elemental cards

These cards show you that 'home' is not anywhere on this physical 'reality' world. Home is not in any dream. Home is where the heart is.
 The heart is your universe where you are the co-creator. Your the dreamer.

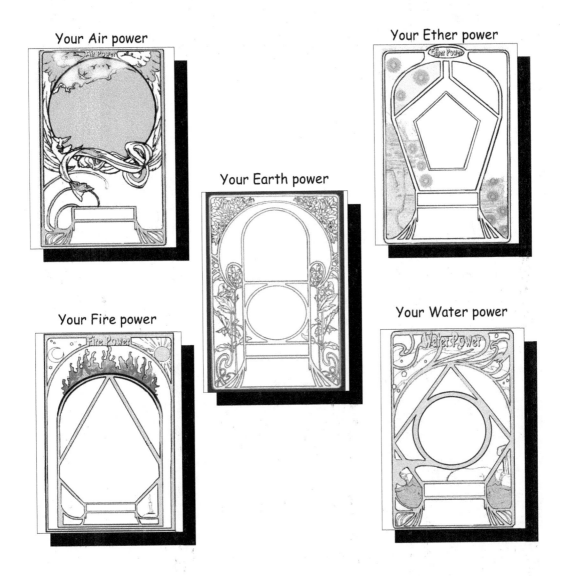

The Earth Element

The 10th Language of Light Quality

Your body awareness that is connected to the element of Earth

The Language of Light quality of <u>Peaceful Bliss</u> is experienced when you surrender to the planet's gravity. People who are mostly in their heads are inclined to float. Allow yourself to surrender by doing a grounding exercise shifting your awareness to the plant kingdom. Visualise your own safe and private space. This sacred space must often be visited during dream time. When you go to bed, have the intent to travel to this sacred space. Many people start to interact with trees because their observation point has shifted. As we touch, or hug or stroke a tree, you have connected with the DNA of the tree. Suddenly during dream time you could start to interact with trees. Richard's great aunt Nadia shared with me how she experienced this connection with the Big tree in the Eastern Cape of South Africa.

Guidelines

- Stay focussed on your sacred space. This can be a special garden, in the mountains, in a valley. Once you have the vision make yourself at home. Keep holding your attention on this special spot. Ask your body avatar to assist and feel your connection with the planet.
- Feel the quality of <u>Peaceful Bliss</u> spreading all over you.
- As you take up your drawing pencils, stay in your vision and with your <u>non-dominant</u> hand draw your feelings out on paper.
- Allow your observer to be the artist.

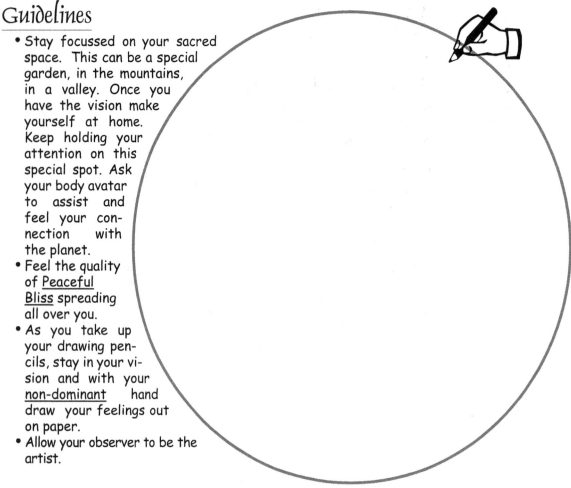

The Earth Element 165

Your Language of Light Card of <u>Peaceful Bliss</u>

Repeat your Language of Light symbol of Peaceful Bliss in the circle within your card. With this **10th** frequency the soul carries the gift of grounding to Spirit into the new paradigm.

Tip

When you have finished, have two colour copies made of your 11th Language of Light card, reduce it to a business card size. Paste one in your Language of Light card at the back of the workbook in the booklet section and laminate the other

Body awareness through the element of Earth

Earth power.

This source of energy comes from the planet itself. Through our last mind-drawing we absorb Earth power through our receptive non dominant hand. For most people that is their left hand.

Earth power is divided into four main divisions. **Earth, Water, Air and Fire.**

Our personal power is usually released from our projective (dominant hand) If you are ambidextrous, use either hand.

All the energy that we use to keep our reality real stems from one universal source.

People who lack earth power usually have a weak Base Chakra. They have difficulty in manifesting or managing money etc. If we express ourselves healthily through this seat of consciousness we are well grounded. That is absolutely the first requirement on your resurrection journey. Ungrounded people have difficulty settling into a stable lifestyle.

Earth power & personal power.

- Choose any one of the other four Language of Light <u>Base Chakra</u> qualities you feel drawn to that you have not embodied through your first name, and write the numeral energy of this quality in the corner of your mind-drawing.
- Breath deeply and visualise how your energy cord is drawing the Earth power up into your Base Chakra.
- Take your dominant hand and again travel back to your sacred space. Allow for your higher self(your observer) to communicate to your body avatar and make the intent to disperse any fear based thought forms.

The Earth Element 167

Your Earth Power card

- The Hexahedron shape of a box is associated with our sense of smell.
- As you creatively start to draw your Language of Light quality symbol of Peaceful Bliss (or other), combine it with your personal power and draw your Earth card. Ground yourself through your Base Chakra while you visualise a shimmery stream of red energy connecting down into the ground with our planet
- Bring into your thought all the good feelings that you associate with nature, planet Earth and yourself.
- Fill in your date of Birth and your sun sign.
- Scale this card down the same way as all the others and laminate it.

Date of Birth..............................
My sun sign........................ ....

The Water Element

The 11th Language of Light Quality

Your body awareness that is connected to the element of Water

The Language of Light quality of <u>Direction</u> is experienced when a new awareness of our individual sexuality is well centred. Our self expression is often enriched by experiencing an orgasm that gets us in touch with a deep sense of joy. Most of our negative programming has resulted in an unacceptable approach to sexual pleasure or expressing ourselves sensually and creatively. Lack of self-expression at this level is the basis for the majority of our disease. A rejection of our physical body is a rejection of ourselves. Most people who do not have a sense of Direction in their lives have a blocked Sacral Chakra, which is related to the water element (our essence of life).

Guideline

- As we ask for a Direction in our lives, we have to trust that our soul is willing to surrender the negative programming that is still within our energy field.
- Again it is all in the intent. We have to address the body avatar and consciously release our distorted belief patterns surrounding our sexuality.
- We cannot raise our kundilini (life force) energy up through the chakras if this level of consciousness is blocked.
- Get in touch with your sexuality from an acceptance of unconditional love for the self when you draw this symbol.

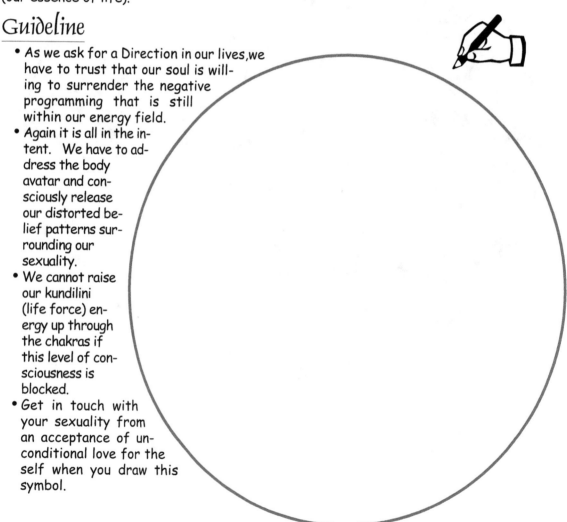

The Water Element 171

Your Language of Light Card of <u>Direction</u>

Repeat the Language of Light symbol of Direction in the circle within your card. With this **11th** frequency the soul carries the gift of surrender to Spirit into the new paradigm.

Tip

When you have finished, have two colour copies made of your 11th Language of Light card, reduce it to a business card size and paste one in your Language of Light card at the back of the workbook in the booklet section. Laminate the other

Body awareness through the element of Water

Water power

The element of Water is the essence of all life on our planet. It often feels as if our emotions are blocked in the Solar Plexus but that is because most people struggle with the first two Chakras. When our personal power is distorted, limited or even nonexistent due to a blocked Sacral Chakra our emotional body lacks psychic energy.

To increase your visual awareness, call upon your psychic mind at will. Imagine what it would be like if you can direct your personal power into a leaf or a plant as you give it water. As the water is soaked up by the soil and the leaves are washed down, your personal power energy mixes with the psychic-inducing power of the water.

Every time you drink a glass of water let your mind dwell on the magic power of our oceans, rivers, lakes, waterfalls, ponds and rainfalls.

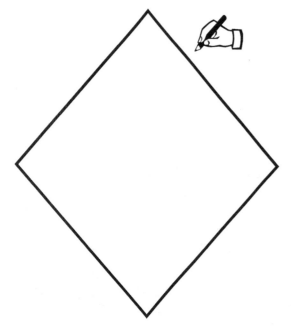

Water power & personal power.

- If you already have the gift of direction, choose any one of the other four Language of Light Sacral chakra qualities that you have not embodied yet through your first name, and write the numeral energy of this quality in the corner of your mind-drawing in the diamond format.
- First breathe deeply and visualise how your Sacral chakra is washed with water power.
- Take your dominant hand and travel back to your sacred space. Add a lake, river, waterfall or pond to your sacred space.
- Allow for your higher self; your observer to communicate to your body avatar and make the intent to disperse any unloving thought forms towards the self.

Your Water Power card

- The Icosahedron shape is associated with the our sense of taste.
- As you creatively start to draw your Language of Light quality symbol of Direction as your water power and combine it with your personal power, draw in your Water card.
- Give yourself your unconditional love through your Sacral chakra while you visualise the power of the oceans on our planet
- Bring into your thought all the good feelings that you associate with water and yourself.
- Fill in your date of Birth and your sun sign.

The Element of Fire

The 12th Language of Light Quality

Your body awareness that is connected to the element of Fire

The Language of Light quality of Hope is experienced when you begin to develop your personal power. You are now able to manifest your dreams. If your dreams are not yet manifesting, look back at the two first observation points. When we are upset we are halting the body's natural emotional synthesizing process. Our Solar Plexus is related to the emotion of anger. Observe if you are expressing anger outwardly or are you suppressing your anger inwardly. If this consciousness awareness centre is healthy we have a high self esteem and a natural ability to manifest abundance on all levels.

Fire is the element of transformation but it is a destructive as well as a creative element. Our observation point is now able to perceive large undertakings on a mundane level. On a spiritual level you can perceive the possibility of physical ascension.

Guidelines

- On this level many people are drawn to transform themselves. Our dream times are vivid and we are developing psychic powers that have been dormant.
- We are now shifting our perception when we are suddenly confronted with new ideas that support the new paradigm.
- We don't consciously hang on to old programming. We feel that there is HOPE to make this world a better place for all.
- Visit your sacred space and light a fire. Visualize a healing ceremony and as you are drawing, mentally look directly into the flames.

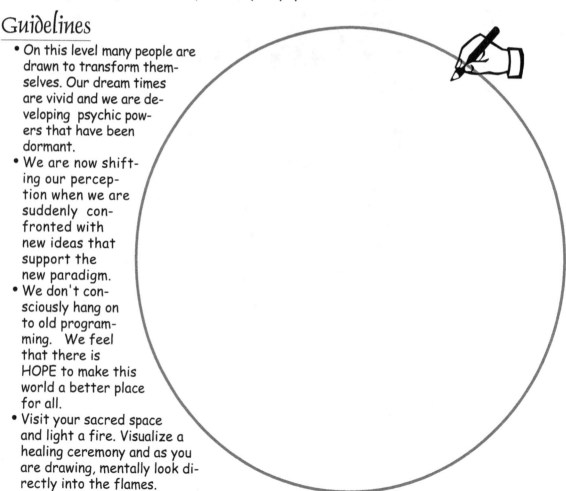

The Element Of Fire 177

Your Language of Light Card of <u>Hope</u>

Repeat the Language of Light symbol of Hope in the circle within your card. With this **12th** frequency the soul carries the gift of having an intent to transform any dis-unity energies. This energy of Hope is necessary to embody amongst the turbulence of today in order to awaken from the illusion and follow Spirit into the new paradigm.

Body awareness through the element of Fire

Fire power

The element of <u>Fire</u> is the creative force that attracts the soul into our body. This conscious awareness centre is the seat of the soul. Often when our personal power is distorted, limited or even nonexistent due to a blocked Sacral Chakra, the fire energy is manifesting as an emotion of anger in our Solar Plexus. This can lead to all kinds of dis-ease to do with our stomach, digestion or disorders and even gall stones. To increase our awareness through this Fire element, visualize yourself as a psychic person. Call upon the sun to energise your whole body. Feel the rays of the sun burning your energies of stored anger away. Use the qualities of forgiveness (base) and freedom (crown) to disperse any blocked thought forms within your auric field. Use the lower mind to contact your psychic mind.

People who have a healthy Solar Plexus are very creative, inventive and enterprising, they develop a healthy relationship with themselves.

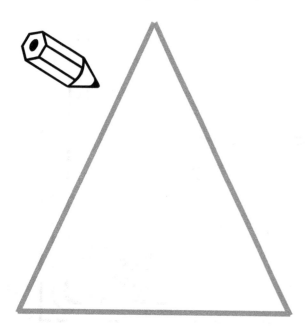

Fire power & personal power.

- Choose any one of the other four Language of Light Solar Plexus qualities that you have not yet embodied through your first name, and write the numeral energy of this quality in the corner of your mind-drawing in the triangle format.
- Visualise how your Solar Plexus chakra is baked in loving energy that burns away any guilt, anger, disappointments that have affected your nervous system.
- Take your dominant hand and again travel back to your sacred space. Add a roaring campfire so your higher self; your observer can disperse of any unloving thought forms towards the self
- Use you sensitivity in all your interaction with others.

Your Fire Power card

- The Tetrahedron shape is associated with our sight, recognition and consciousness.
- As you start to draw your Language of Light quality symbol of Hope, combine it with visions that reflects Hope to you.
- Visualise a roaring fire and go into the flame.
- Bring into your thought all the good feelings that you associate with this flame of purification.
- Fill in your date of Birth and your sun sign.
- Scale this card down the same way as all the others and laminate it.

The Element of Air

The 13th Language of Light Quality

Your body awareness that is connected to the element of Air

Divine union is experienced when the Heart chakra is activated. This <u>Divine Union</u> is like having a love affair with oneself. It's through our breathing that our Heart Chakra anchors our life force in an upwards movement. Our observation point of perception starts to shift outside our auric field as we use various breathing techniques. This gives us a universal view toward our life experience instead of an individual one.

Because of the expansion of awareness that has opened up, this vortex acts like a bridge. Only transformed creative and healthy energy is allowed to pass this energy centre. Our observation point is also tremendously enhanced by the quality and amount of air we inhale and exhale.

Any addictions become downgraded to preferences and we begin to find that we can instantly accept what was previously emotionally unacceptable. Now you are aware that feelings of isolation and separation are always artificially created by our emotional programming.

On this level your time will usually be spent with people who have similar preferences and with whom you enjoy doing things.

Guidelines

- As you travel towards your sacred space, see your higher self meeting you halfway.
- The expression of unconditional love shines from her or his face as you come closer.
- You are welcomed into the heart of your sacred space by a loved one.
- Birds are singing, water is tricking down while a smouldering fire awaits you.
- Beauty is everywhere.
- As you take up your drawing tools you are experiencing a Divine Union with the self.

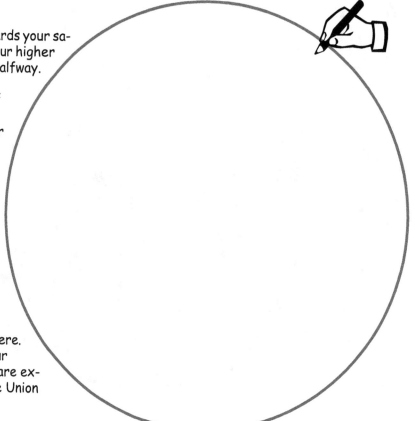

The Element Of Air 183

Your Language of Light Card of <u>Divine Union</u>

Repeat your Language of light symbol of Divine Union in the circle within your card. With this **8th** frequency the soul carries the gift of unconditional love for all life to Spirit into the new paradigm.

Tip

When you have finished, have two colour copies made of your 11th Language of Light card, reduce it to a business card size and paste one in your Language of Light card at the back of the workbook in the booklet section. And laminate the other

Body awareness through the element of Air

Air power

As you are embodying the Quality of <u>Divine Union</u>, you will prepare yourself for a truly loving relationship like Ingrid and Toon have with each other. The new expansion of your heart chakra will allow the energy to flow more dynamically out to the other chakras.

On this level of consciousness we will 'fall in love' and take the energy down to our solar plexus chakra and synthesize it. Ideally, we then take it down to our sexual chakra and express ourselves sensually/sexually to our beloved. We then allow the energy to flow to our Base Chakra and put down roots. We blend with the earth element and some of us start a family. Our inner attitudes about our self is often reflected in the people we draw into our lives. Many of us do not believe that we deserve, or are good enough to manifest happiness joy, love and abundance.

This was a hard one for me but I now know that I can experience anything I want.

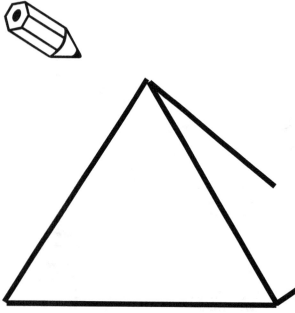

Air power & personal power.

- Choose any one of the other eight Language of Light Heart Chakra qualities that you felt attracted to but have not embodied yet through your first name vibrations, and write the numeral energy of this quality in the corner of your mind-drawing.
- Breathe deeply and visualise how your energy vortex is slowly starting to spin.
- Take your dominant hand and again travel back to your sacred space. You are not alone, your higher self is waiting for you.
- Together you will travel further on this journey of awakening.
- Feel the air elemental energy all round you. You are crossing the bridge into eternity.

Your Air Power card

- The Octahedron shape is associated with sound, (listening) the bird kingdom pyramid healing and the colour yellow.
- As you creatively start to draw your Language of Light quality symbol of Divine Union as your air power and combine it with your extra personal power symbol, create your Air card.
- Visualise that your guide (higher self) has joined you.
- Bring into your thoughts all the good feelings that you associate with a loving relationship.
- Fill in your date of Birth and your sun sign.
- Scale this card down the same way as all the others and laminate it.

The Element of Ether

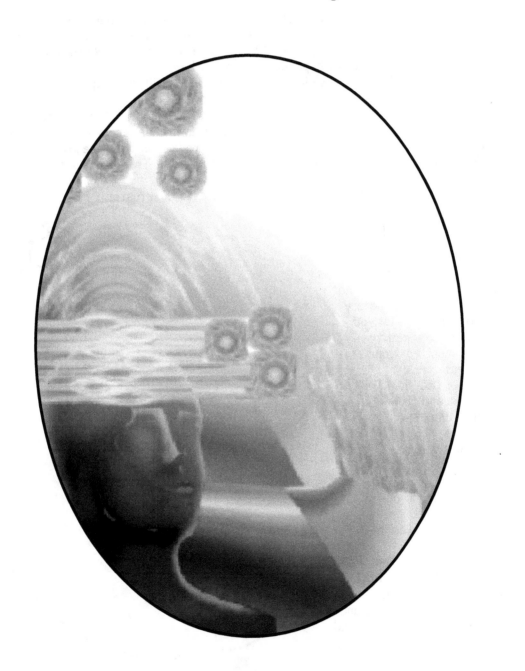

The 14th Language of Light Quality

Your body awareness that is connected to the element of Ether

This is the fifth point of observation from where we can shift our perception of this world anyway we want. You will experience life more and more in the Love centre of consciousness. You will find friendships that you could never have found before. You will begin to experience your life as one miraculous happening after another.

You will begin to feel that you live in a friendly world that will always give you 'enough'. You feel at home anywhere.

When you are eating, your food is enjoyed from the love centre. Your etheric template, your light body, is ready to fully receive your conscious awareness as your body's put to rest. You will become the dreamer. You are fully aware that while asleep you are in a dream within a dream. You can now explore the vast regions of your soul field. The illusion of 'Time' does not apply anymore.

Your chakras, when all in balance, will start to spin faster and faster.

Guidlines

- The 14th Language of Light quality is the gift of <u>Abundance.</u> This quality does not meant that you now receive monetary rewards, it means that you have the energy and the power to manifest your Soul Purpose.
- If you have the 'intent' to ascend from this third dimensional realm, You will receive all the assistance you need and more.
- Abundance means access to unlimited creative psychic power to manifest.
- While you draw out the gift of abundance, go to your sacred space, your higher self will greet you and take you on a multidimensional tour.

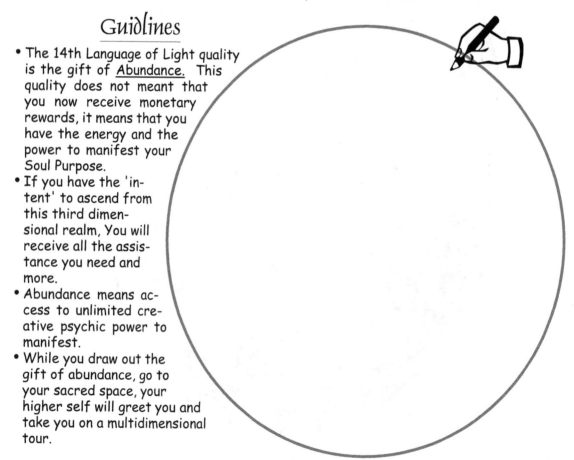

Your Language of Light Card of <u>Abundance</u>

Repeat your Language of Light symbol of <u>Abundance</u> in the circle within your card. With this **14th** frequency.
The soul carries the gift of unlimited creative power to Spirit into the new paradigm.

Abundance

My own Symbol of Light

Body awareness through the element of Ether

The ETHER element we are referring to is a medium through which electromagnetic waves are transmitted into a higher frequency. From this level of consciousness this element can appear as a light, airy, highly delicate substance. The lower Astral realm is completely etheric.

The astral realm has at least seven levels according to Annelies. We mostly visit the lower realms in our dreams.

That is where inorganic beings are very eager to interact with human consciousness, especially when the dreamer is not aware. The moment you become 'aware' you travel to higher astral realms. Richard explains about the different astral realms in his journals: **The Astral Explorer** and **The Cosmic Traveller**.

From this level of consciousness we gradually awaken to a higher awareness

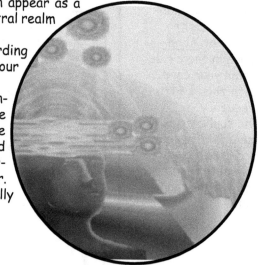

Attaining a fifth-dimensional awareness allows us to fully embody unconditional love and unconditional acceptance of all other life-forms on the face of the Earth. In order to accomplish this, all emotional records of pain, abuse, shame, anger, and fear must be erased from the cellular structure of our entire embodiment.

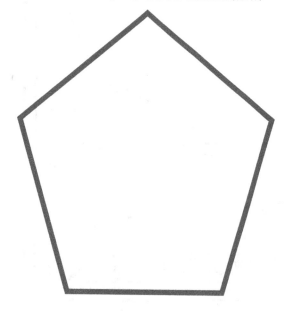

Ether power & personal power.

- Choose any one of the other eight Language of Light Crown Chakra qualities, or any of the three Throat Chakra qualities that you felt attracted to but have not embodied yet through your first name vibrations, and write the numeral energy of this quality in the corner of your mind-drawing.
- Close your eyes and visualise what the energy looks like of the Language of Light quality you chose to embody.
- Draw your own symbol of that quality into the Dodecahedron shape.
- Feel the life force travelling up your spine past your throat chakra. Take a deep breath and push your energy into your Third Eye.

Your Ether Power card

The Element Of Ether 191

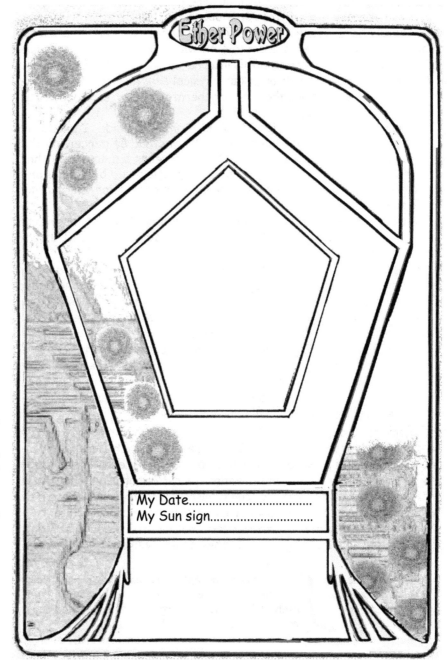

The Dodecahedron shape is associated with the sense of touch and Spirit. The colour violet is often seen in auric fields of people that have awakened to this level of consciousness.

As you start to draw your Language of Light quality symbol of Abundance within your Ether power card combine it with your personal power.

Visualise your kundaliny energy rising up through your spinning chakras

Fill in your date of Birth and your sun sign.
Scale this card down the same way as all the others and laminate it.

My Date..............................
My Sun sign..........................

Closure

The following interpretations from all the mind-drawing exercises are derived from the personal assessments my students shared with me over a period of a few years. I also acquired a great deal of knowledge about colour therapy through the Anthroposophical association in Utrecht during the nineties. I have used the 7 major energy vortices to create a personal awareness scale to ascertain on which level of the conscious awareness the soul is partaking in this incarnation. These vibrational wave bands that we experience through our physical senses as colours, movement, shapes and sounds are the body's generator system can speak to us through our mind-drawings.

Through my interaction with POWAH, Annelies' guide, I gradually started to learn to perceive energy directly, instead of perceiving the world as concrete physical objects. Over the years I discovered that each individual is only partly unique and partly influenced by beliefs and likes and dislikes when it comes to colour. Our attraction for certain colours seems to change as we grow in awareness.

Especially when it comes to colours; people seem to react; providing I take their age and gender into consideration similarly when I interpret their art work.

- Shapes, line and texture are expressions from the present moment. Each moment is an opportunity to capture the language of the body, mind, spirit.
- When mind-drawings take on a pattern, they start to reveal an energy that could be labelled, so to speak.
- Symbols reveal feelings, especially when your interpretations are guided by the seven conscious awareness levels combined with the five creative stages in which the analogue drawing formats were created.
- Each chakra level has a certain vibration that influences our perceptions, even if a mixture of colours has been used.

Many people tried out the formats before I was certain that they were a safe space for their thought-forms to be processed through. During our resurrection process we all will occasionally drop back into the lower awareness levels only to heal and release mis-creations of our own making. This dream world is here for us to enjoy, but we can totally enjoy it only when we are free from identifying with the illusionary roles we play in the drama of life.

With the help of Annelies, we created the Chakra, Language of Light, and the Elemental cards together, so they could later be used in her ascension board game.

> "If we stop perceiving ourselves as egos, accepting instead that we are fields of energy, then we will change our view of reality, and our behaviour in it. As egos we need to defend ourselves. As fields of energy we are concerned about the appropriate use of energy, that is with impeccability."
>
> VictorSanchez, The Teachings of Don Carlos

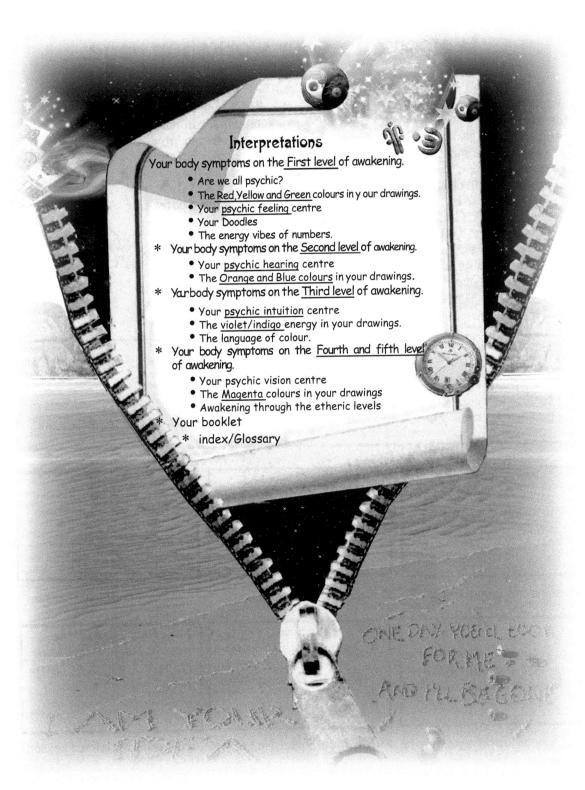

Interpretations

Your body symptoms on the <u>First level</u> of awakening.

- Are we all psychic?
- The <u>Red, Yellow and Green</u> colours in your drawings.
- Your <u>psychic feeling</u> centre
- Your Doodles
- The energy vibes of numbers.

* Your body symptoms on the <u>Second level</u> of awakening.

  - Your <u>psychic hearing</u> centre
  - The <u>Orange and Blue colours</u> in your drawings.

* Your body symptoms on the <u>Third level</u> of awakening.

  - Your <u>psychic intuition</u> centre
  - The <u>violet/indigo</u> energy in your drawings.
  - The language of colour.

* Your body symptoms on the <u>Fourth and fifth level</u> of awakening.

  - Your psychic vision centre
  - The <u>Magenta</u> colours in your drawings
  - Awakening through the etheric levels

* Your booklet
  * index/Glossary

Welcome to your workshop page.

It really does not require a trained eye to see the difference between fast and slow talking people. It does not require an expert in handwriting to recognise if you are an extrovert outgoing person or an introvert reserved person. Your handwriting is a line drawing that reflects your personal temperament. When you wrote your address on the envelope on page..., you already did a mind-drawing.

Graphology is an exciting and useful key to aid in unlocking the potential within you. Under the Biography I have listed some hand writing titles that guided me through my mind-drawing studies.

It is very appropriate to start looking at your welcome page, because due to our computers and word processors many people hardly ever write by hand anymore.

- **Margins** reveal a great deal about the writer. It shows what degree of tolerance or consistency YOU the writer has. Look back at your welcome page.
- Does your writing have a wide left or right or up or down margin?
- Is your writing style slanted to the right or left?
- Do you use up all the space, or are you frugal or use as little as possible?

I am interested in the art analogue course because I want to learn who I am.	I am interested in the art analogue course because I want to learn who I am.	I am interested in the art analogue course because I want to learn who I am.
Running away from the self?	This could be an early riser?	An aloof or lonely person

I am interested in the art-analogue drawing because I want to	I am interested in the art-analogue drawing because I want to learn about who I am	I am interested in the art-analogue drawing because I want to learn about who I am
Secrecy or lack of spontaneity	An impatient impulsive person?	Very self-disciplined person?

Interpretations 197

Your signature is the most personal line drawing that reveals your self-image which shows if you are a creative and intuitive or an analysing and intellectual or a secret and/ or shy person.
It's all revealed in the slant, letter spacing, strokes and the size and pressure you use when you write your signature.

> *[Handwritten sample: "I would like to first have an understanding of Art-Analogue Symbolism. I have never practiced any form of Art & have No knowledge of any aspect of it. I know its a Creative talent & thats it!"]*

Judy's slant in her writing is backwards which indicates that her thoughts are more occupied with her past. It reveals an early rejection in childhood. The strokes and the angles reflect a creative and idealistic person with a very neat and controlling streak.

Any handwriting has both positive and negative traits and you must never jump to conclusions, but it's your intuitive faculty that can read between the lines and letters what person you are dealing with.

Having a variety of samples will give far more information but I will share some of my welcome sheets with you to give you an idea what you can already observe without knowing the person at all.

Henny is not a great talker. She is both reserved and unsure of herself, but there is an artist lurking behind the persona. Her wide spacings are indicating that she has a cautious but philosophical nature. Her signature goes uphill so her outlook in life is positive.

> *[Handwritten sample: "I would like to be able to express my creative self. To awaken the artist/creator within me."]*

> *[Handwritten sample: "I want to learn to draw! The next level of my personal development is to learn to express myself creatively. Basic drawing skills would form a solid & firm foundation from which to explore other creative expression. THANK YOU FOR THIS OPPORTUNITY!"]*

Jill is a very strong willed woman who knows what she wants but her willfulness scare many people away. That creates a loneliness so she goes within. Like Henny's signature Jill also slants upwards. Both have the staying power to see things through no matter what.

The Seven Centres of Consciousness

The interpretations from this workbook are guided by the 7 human consciousness awareness levels. These vibrational wave bands that we experience through our physical senses as visions, colours, shapes, movement, texture, aroma and sounds, activate our psychic abilities, talents, gifts and endurance to experience what it is like to be human. The 7 major chakras also emanate twenty-one minor vortices as well as forty still smaller spinning energy funnels, ejecting still smaller ones, but they are not found in the physical body. They relate to our subtle etheric bodies which is beyond the scope of this workbook.

You will already have grown in awareness while following the workbook, for this reason I will share my gathered information, which was derived from many sources, how we all have a lot in common, and how unique we are as well.

Are we all Psychic?

Our first Psychic feeling centres

Most people are psychic in this area but don't know it. Although our entire body is a feeling antenna, the focal point lies in the abdomen from the top of the diaphragm to just below the navel near the Solar Plexus which is our master antenna.

Tuning ourselves to the higher octaves of Light and changing our vibrational frequency has been explored extensively in the previous chapters, but again I must warn you that the process of transition into Light is a gradual one.

We are not matter one day and pure Light the next. Our energy fields are gradually infused and more realigned to a higher frequency or else we would experience electrical 'burn out'.

The mind-drawing from your Base and Solar Plexus displays your ability to cope in this world and how your personal security issues influence your life.

This can range from your financial status, your place in our community, your nutritional intake and the physical security worries you might harbour in your energy field.

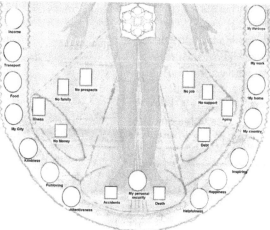

Interpretation

Your Base field drawing with the number scale will show you the level of intensity or concern that occupies your unconscious mind on a daily basis.

This information was gathered through all the first level exercises in this workbook.

Most of us can relate to our way of rating something through giving it a number. For most of us the higher the number the more intense the feelings.

Look back at your drawings on the first level and fill in the **total** numeral scale on personal and fear based issues next to the Base funnel and what your total rating is on your inspirations and admiration levels above and below the figure

- Any added number that passes a total of **50** in the two circles below the large one then you must know that there are plenty of security issues that keeps you from awakening. Your fear levels are high.
- Any number below 50 and you are well on your way to let go of fear based programming.

If the numbers you placed in the two circles top and bottom of the figure pass the **30** mark you are an active well adjusted individual who will find your soul purpose if you have not already.

My admiration scale

Our Psychic Feeling Centre

My total score of all the four vibration levels.

My anxiety on security   My fear based score

My inspiration scale

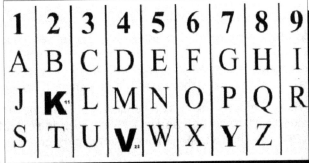

Your total score in the large circle often reveals how you rate yourself from a physical point of view. If your score is below this number you have to look again at the things you can be grateful for in your life.

Read up on the Red colour ray and the symbols that were expressed in Red in your mind-drawings. Look within and allow your memories to surface into your conscious mind in order to release them.

Your body symptoms on the First level of awakening.

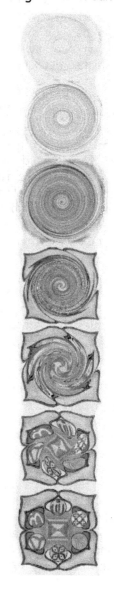

When the body drops density due to our awakening, it commonly displays mutational symptoms of flu, headaches, diarrhea, rashes, muscle and joint aches. Most flu epidemics are actually Light epidemics! Because we start to work on ourselves and we start to shift perceptions and our brain chemistry changes. Our right and left brain functions blend more and more due to the mind-drawing exercises and the pituitary and pineal glands begin to change in size.

The DNA structure and chemical components begin to change and pick up extra hydrogen atoms and chemicals that the cells need to take undifferentiated higher Light and break it down into a useable Light encodement for the DNA.

We are all evolving and absorbing Light at our own pace. Some are consciously working with these changes and so their transmutation is quicker, some are unaware and are absorbing this Light and change in direct relation to planetary change. However, one can classify this creation into five levels.

When our etheric blueprint floods with light and releases karmic experiences, many people may feel disoriented as well as experience 'bouts of flu'. Many begin to question "why am I here". Light restructuring from the 4th dimensional etheric blueprint causes spins in the geometries of the emotional, mental and spiritual bodies. Change is rapid and many feel tired.

As you see by the spinning Base Chakra, the speed at which it operates goes along with the feelings that reflect the following:

Unhappiness, which is a psychological state arises when life repeatedly gives us what we do not want to accept. This is what is called **Addictive programmed mind-sets**. These fear-based thought-forms are tied up with our emotional responses produced in the limbic areas of our organic brain. Most of our population is consciously aware on the first Base Chakra without any of the Language of Light qualities.

As we embody the first 6 Language of Light qualities the Base Chakra can start to spin. The first three speeds reflect the stage of our awakening. Then we opened our heart chakra and we are on our journey.

Happiness, which is a psychological state, arises from experiencing frequent pleasure. Often this happy space comes to us when we are learning to accept. We have started to use **Preferential programming** by allowing the energy flow to flow in the 'here and now'. There is no connection made regarding our emotional fears through our thoughts. We have reprogrammed our rational mind not to connect the fulfilment or lack of fulfilment with the limbic areas.

From now on we gather all the addictive mind-sets from all the other conscious awareness centres. We start to feel lighter and we interact with people who are on a similar wave length.

Often during our resurrection process we will now and then drop back in density in order to gather mind-sets that were left behind.

All the centres have to be in balance, so if we have mind-sets locked in our Solar Plexus or in our Heart centre, we stay below the third or fourth level for as long as it takes. Some people leave this life in order to incarnate again and go through the process again. But this time they are faster.

That is why there are so many young people who seem to awaken very early. They will become the leaders when we have moved fully into the new paradigm.

Bliss, is a state of continuous happiness. **Bliss programming** permits us to achieve a state of awareness that life is not related to any variable life realities. You are living in the absolute joy of the moment. This is the fourth into the 5th awareness level. This does not mean that we are unaware of destructive behaviour, pain, hurt or despair in others. There will always be opposite polarities in this illusionary dream. We will just not feed them!

True compassion is letting the other _be_ and love them unconditionally regardless of their awareness level. When one sees the bigger picture, there is no more blame.

Let's explore your Psychic _feeling_ centres again

The Green Heart energy colour channel

The Red Base/ Root energy colour channel

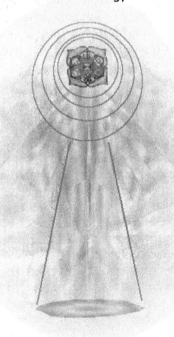

The Yellow Solar Plexus energy colour channel

Most people are Psychically aware but don't know it. Although our entire body is a feeling antenna, the focal point lies in the abdomen from the top of the diaphragm to just below the navel near the Solar Plexus.

Yellow and Green in your drawings on the First consciousness level.

If you have **not** used any of these three colours during the first and second exercise then there is a lot of grounding work to be done with the Base Chakra. You are not active in the psychic feeling region.

- Look at your symbols within your drawings. Link them with any security issues you might have.
- Are your colours strong and vibrant? That could mean that your physical energy is high.
- Do you have a lot of yellow in your drawings? That could mean that you are a lot in your head but it does suggest an active mind.
- A preference for the colour yellow in most drawings suggest that this person is drawn to new modern technology.
- If you have both red, green and yellow in your drawings on the exercises surrounding our psychic feeling centre, you are psychic in that area. You listen to your body. Become aware of your body language when you feel uncomfortable. Keep asking yourself, "Why do I feel bad? Or, why does that feel good?"

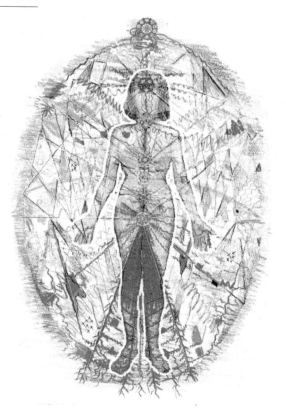

When Our Solar Plexus still has a mind set that holds on to the feelings of not being good enough, not getting approval, or a great lack of self esteem, those distorted thought forms are blockages from our Sacral and Solar Plexus chakras that controls the lower mental body. Our unconscious translates and stores these genuine emotional fears in our rational mind.

Fearful thoughts that we have inherited from our caretakers (parents) and even genetically inherited beliefs are also programmed addictions that have a great effect on our lives. Those negative energies in our field can even effect our receptor organ of sight, plus our kinesthetic sense which sends millions of impulses per second towards our organic computer.

Psychic feelers are the most sensitive to the feelings of others. They are flexible and the best at adapting to keep everyone happy.

Our psychic feeling awareness will greatly improve once our Heart chakra is activated. If all three lower chakras are in balance, we can become medical intuitives or healers.

Our physical senses become much stronger. Our bodies not only absorb Light for its own change but also acts as a transducer- decoder of higher light energies to the planet as a whole. The process of ascension is now irreversible.

The Red, Yellow and Green colour energies in your drawings.

(Regretfully this workbook was printed in a grey scale. An e-book version in full colour can be obtained through the website of the publisher or the author(see our imprint page)

The interpretations from the workbook are guided by the 7 human consciousness awareness levels that are activated during the five creative stages in our lives. We experience these energy channels through our physical senses as visions, colours, shapes, movement, texture, aroma and sounds. These 7 chakras emanate twenty-one minor vortices as well as forty still smaller spinning energy funnels, ejecting still smaller ones. They are not found in the physical body but they relate to our subtle etheric bodies.

The gift of your Will power

Stage one

This first awareness level is guided by the Red ray whose quality activates the <u>will power</u> in man.
- The archetype from the tarot deck, **The Empire,**
- The astrological personality type of **Aries,**
- The energy of planet **Mars is reflected in our mind-drawing**
- The elements of **Fire/ Earth**, all guide us for our physical ascension, if so intended.

Awakening through the Base Chakra (your security centre)

As you read the interpretations on red, yellow and green, look at your first mind drawings on page:30 and 31.

The colour **Red** in drawings often seem to deal with issues that are from our past. If emotional expressions and feelings are drawn out with the colour red, it often reveals that the thoughts on this wavelength are dragged out of our memory files from deep within. It is an almost primal male energy.

- **Dark red** can indicate a high temper or some nervous turmoil. This person can be domineering and quick to act.
- A deep **maroon red** can also mean sensuality.
- If the colour red is very light in the first two drawings it often reveals a very active but impulsive person.
- A lot of **Pink** in the first mind drawing often reflects some immaturity or naivety in the person.
- Clear, **bright pink** bespeaks human affection that has been softened by sorrow.

The colour Red is the energy that activates our life force.

- A lack of red in a drawing could be a lack of energy, someone that lacks the male energy or in some drawings, depending on the exercise, it can reveal that we are urged to start something new.
- Red in a drawing can also be a testing period or in some exercises to means the will to thrive.

Some people will use red as a colour that expresses to them having confidence, believing in themselves or something they are not frightened of. It all depends on the drawing exercise. When you study your own drawings, listen to your body. What level of energy are you aware of. Is it heavy, strong, hot, or emotional.

Red energy is flowing in this drawing. The darker lines are a strong red with orange and green. The yellow in the centre reveals that the person was accessing his thoughts through the solar plexus.

The moving curved lines indicates the man (artist) has a feminine nature. He wrote the feeling words of warm, comforting, alive.

As you can see the whole space has been used to express the feelings surrounding a meal. This indicates that the time the meal was taking place was well balanced and happy

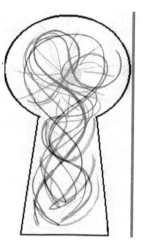

The often hidden message in an art-analogue mind-drawing symbols are very personal. No one can really know what is in another's Soul consciousness, but when you study your own drawings the hidden meanings could trigger a message from your higher Self

RED for Hildegard von Bingen expressed the zealous, justice seeking impulse born from God within.

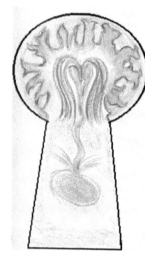

- Red can also mean that you are committed to life, the will to survive and the acceptance of the body-fire of emotion. Making Red your first choice in some drawings can indicate an urge towards success, intense experiences, and a full life.
- Rejecting Red in some drawings can suggest that you already feel overstimulated and you are seeking to protect yourself from experiences likely to bring further excitement or aggravation.
- **Reddish-brown** indicates avarice, greed or selfishness we are hiding within.
- **Scarlet** reveals an over-abundance of personal pride.
- **Carmine**- a clear pure red denotes strength, endurance and a high state of physical perfection.
- Red is also the symbol for sacrifice, it has positive meanings that suggest the energy we need to survive, be healthy and transform ourselves to greater inner wisdom.
- When Red is mixed with another colour (purple, orange, or pink) it suggest that energy is present but strongly bound up with whatever is symbolized by the colour with which the red colour is blended.

At first glance one would think that the meal was hot and spicy. You can almost taste the drawing. The symbol of the heart surrounded by orange fire, with the green ball that is surrounded by yellow and blue speaks of a good time! I know that both the people who drew these keyhole drawings on this page had a meal together. They are a couple deeply in love! How different did she express her feelings surrounding their dinner.

Your Hidden Symbols in Red

CIRCLES in our drawings
- The circle is widely accepted as a symbol for eternity, but with the Red circle the meaning is often only known by the individual.
- Time is associated with this symbol. It means the beginning of something.
- A solid red round ball or balls in a drawing contains lots of emotions.

CROSSES, LIMES, OR HEAVY MARKS
- Any uneven crosses, lines or strong marks reveal a strong, sometimes angry emotion.
- Depending on the drawing exercise, any crosses mean hidden feelings are stirred.
- Any red arrows in drawings and you wonder at whom they are pointing.
- A cross can also symbolise a state of mind. It can mark a special place, or it can mean the person is dealing with life's difficulties and is at a crossroad.
- Any dots or stipples again in red could mean a strong viewpoint that is not verbally expressed.

RED FIVE POINTED STARS in drawings often indicate a well-grounded person.

HEARTS are mostly symbols of love, however, the red heart may also represent spiritual fervour.

SQUARES give the impression of firmness.
- Red triangles are also an indicator of direction.

TRIANGLES
- Facing down stands for feminine and facing up masculine.

SPIRALS in drawings often express a longing for wholeness.
- Red spirals can also reflect a strong attachment cord with someone.

FLAGS, SUNS and **FLOWERS** in red often reflect finished business or the birth of a new awareness.

AN INFINITY SIGN in a drawing.

When this sign is used, especially when it is in Red, this symbolizes unlimited time or it talks about an experience in a relationship

A lot can be read from our early exercises when we study our hidden fear drawings. Look at the colours you have chosen for the things you rate high.

Look again at your mind-drawings and an inner language starts to form. The colour vibrations with their shapes and lines are created by our thoughts. They are in constant movement and they give off a sound within our auric energy field, thereby creating the material world we perceive. Remember that I said perceive! As you study your drawings ask yourself, which aspect of me is the observer? Is it my Lower or higher self?

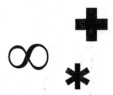

The Yellow energies in your drawing

The Solar Plexus chakra is our power centre and the seat of our lower mental body. This awareness centre controls our status and the ego. This vortex is the subtle centre that influences the activities of digestion and absorption of food. When this channel is 'damaged' we are a slave to our ego. Physical problems in the solar plexus area can therefore relate to the conflict of power and ego-identity issues represented by this chakra. The colour yellow is associated with the adrenal glands.

The gift of our Inner power

Stage one

This third ray's quality activates our intellect by activating our inner power in order to rise above the lower levels of energy represented by the first two chakras.
- The archetype from the tarot deck is The Magician,
- The astrological personality type of Virgo/Capricorn reflects an energy that can be both reflective and receptive.
- The energy Mercury is reflected in our mind-drawings.
- the elements of Fire with Air all guide us to balance our left and Right thinking mode hemispheres.

The colour Yellow in drawings often seems to deal with light and brightness in our lives. In our imageries of light we are using our mental subtle bodies while drawing.

Awakening through the Solar Plexus Chakra (our inner power centre)

DIRTY YELLOW is often associated with negative attachments to difficulties with authority. Again a lot of Yellow in a drawing often reflects a good mind. Yellow in a drawing can reveal feelings of robust energetic well-defined sense of self. Some people will use Yellow when they are ready to learn something new.

YELLOW can sometimes reflect a feeling of a need for change or seeking change for the sake of change. For some people the colour Yellow represents the precious metal of gold. Sometimes our unconscious uses the imagery of gold to remind us that we carry the imprinted potential for wholeness within.

When our energy is blocked in this chakra, we are likely be driven by our inner voice that comes from the ego mind, not the higher mind. Yellow is the energy vortex that stimulates our intellect. Each ray or light has specific qualities which refers, metaphysically speaking, to attributes to the specific manifestation patterns of that energy. Yellow has a mental focussed energy

Your Hidden Symbols in Yellow

CIRCLES in our drawings
- The circle is widely accepted as a symbol for eternity, but with the Yellow circle the meaning is often seen as the symbol of the sun.

ROUND BALLS in drawings
- These symbols are often associated with the illusion of Time. It means the beginning of something new. A solid Yellow round ball or balls in a drawing can contain lots of ideas that is stimulating the mind. The process of personal experiences. wisdom

UNEVEN CROSSES, lines or strong marks in Yellow in drawings.
- These symbolic expression again can sometimes just reflect a hostile attitude towards a father figure. Depending on the drawing exercise, any crosses means hidden feelings that are stirred to do with our sense of inner peace. A Yellow cross in general can also symbolise self knowledge.

ARROWS in drawings.
- Any Yellow arrows in drawings means you must know that they are pointing to new opportunities. Reaching upward means they are pointing towards a higher dimension of awareness.

FLAGS, SUNS AND FLOWERS.
- These are often happy memories in drawings

HEARTS in drawings
- Yellow hearts again are mostly symbols of love, however, the Yellow heart may also represent a spiritual focus.

SQUARES in drawings.
- Squares gives the impression of firmness but they are rarely drawn in Yellow.

TRIANGLES in drawings.
- It they are facing down stands for feminine and facing up masculine.

SPIRALS in drawings.
- In Yellow are often express a longing for order and can reveal the characteristic of a perfectionist.

AN INFINITY SIGN in a drawing,
- When this symbol is especially used in scarlet orange, it symbolizes an intimate time in a relationship experience.

Remember that all the impressions in your drawings that are expressed in this mental colour <u>Yellow</u> is often inclined to be influenced by your linear mode of thinking.

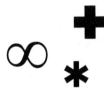

Your Hidden Symbols in Green

The fourth Heart chakra is the centre where compassion rules. To be psychically aware this vortex must be fully activated. This major chakra distributes its rays of love to all the cells and nerve centres in the lower as well as the higher chakras. The Heart centre is where the pink fires of love burn brightly. It is the seat of illumined conscience which you will make your own by love's discernment and wisdom's true discrimination. This vortex is situated at the eighth cervical vertebra, close to the thymus gland.

The gift of Compassion

Level one

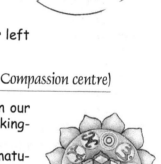

The Green ray connects through the heart to Body, Mind and Spirit.
- The archetype from the tarot deck is The Empress.
- The astrological personality type of Taurus/Cancer reflects an energy that can be both demonstrative and unreserved.
- The energy of Jupiter is reflected in our mind drawings.
- The elements of Earth with Water all guide us to balance our left and Right thinking mode hemispheres.

Awakening through the Heart Chakra (our Compassion centre)

The colour Green in drawings often seems to deal with nature in our lives. In our imageries the feelings of love, healing and the nature kingdom often unconsciously reflect a soul longing for home.

Green in a drawing can signify that one has reached a point in maturity. A lot of Green in a drawing often reflects a warm and compassionate heart. Those people are often already in a helping profession. DARK GREEN in a drawing can reveal feelings of fear that speaks to the memories of a dark forest where the witch lives. Some people will use Green when they are expanding to something new.

Sometimes a great deal of Green reflects memories of being overly controlled by a parent. This in turn can reveal that the person has to overcome the need to be overprotective themselves. Green is the energy vortex that stimulates us into expansion.

To some people the colour green is a symbol of negativity as they associate the poisonous venom of snakes, which is greenish. Each ray or light has specific qualities which refers, metaphysically speaking, to attributes to the specific manifestation patterns of that energy.

Green involves health, expansion, abundance and harmony.

Your Hidden Symbols in Green

CIRCLES in our drawings
- The circle is widely accepted as a symbol for eternity, but with the Green circle the meaning is often seen as the symbol of the expansion. The illusion of time is associated with this symbol. Time plays a large role in the way we perceive this reality. It means the beginning of something new.

ROUND BALLS in drawings
- A solid Green round ball or balls in a drawing can contain lots of feelings towards a person or an idea.

CROSSES in drawings.
- Any uneven crosses, lines or strong marks in Green often reflect nature. Depending on the drawing exercise, any crosses means hidden feelings that are stirred to do with our sense of smell that triggers memories from our childhood. A Green cross in general reveals that the person has a caring heart.

A LOT OF GREEN in a drawing can reveal that a person that has been suppressed by domineering parent(s) and they themselves are overprotective towards their loved ones.

ARROWS.
- Any Green arrows in drawings point to new opportunities, or new ideas. Reaching upward means they are pointing towards a higher dimension of awareness.

HEARTS in drawings
- Green hearts are often drawn by people who are in a caring profession. Squares give the impression of firmness but they are rarely drawn in Green unless they represent the planet.

TRIANGLES
- A triangle facing down stands for feminine and facing up masculine.

SPIRALS in drawings.
- Spirals in Green are often drawn unconsciously, they can be a sign that the soul is longing for home. The person is a seeker and is searching.

AN INFINITY SIGN
- An infinity sign in a drawing, especially when it is scarlet orange, symbolizes an intimate time in a relationship experience.

DARK GREEN can also be a negative reaction to something. It can symbolize a dark bewitched forest.

The shapes in our drawing where Green is most used can reflect that your Heart chakra vortex is activated through the sense of smell.

What is revealed through your doodles?

The box that reveals your Self Image

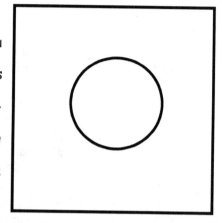

- If you have drawn a flower it's a feminine sign and you care about your surroundings and appearance.
- If you have drawn a charming or comic figure or face it shows a good nature, a sense of humour and you use diplomacy.
- A sun symbol indicates a strong dominant self-confident personality.
- An ugly figure shows that you have difficulty getting close to other people.
- An eye in this drawing means pride. It can also reflect a suspicious nature. You might have to look at your attempt to control your life and your relationships.
- Anything else you have to work out for yourself. (Do you think as yourself as a balloon?)

The box that reveals your Home

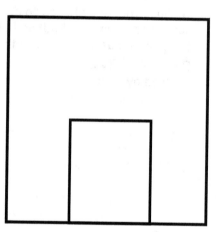

- If you have drawn something inside the box your interest lies in the home.
- If you have drawn something outside the box your interest lies outside the home.
- Unattached people who would like to create a home often may make nest-like symbols(a fire place, a house a window) or they put something inside the box to indicated their idea of a home. (Champagne, glass, bed)
- If you have drawn both inside and outside the box you are ambivalent. (Which is normal)
- If you have made the box a grotesque face it shows you have a fear of a home and/ or a marriage.

The box that reveals your main interest.

- You can work this out for yourself.
- If your have drawn the person of the same sex as you it shows that your main interest is you (and why not)
- Landscapes and still life indicate an artistic ability.
- If you leave the box blank you are either a workaholic and have no time for hobbies, or you should take up a hobby.
- This box really reveals where your attention lies. Unconscious, subconscious or unconscious.

The box that reveals your Friendships

- Drawing many shapes indicates many friends. Most people make several different shapes inside this box.
- Only shapes within the two lines indicate that your friends are restricted to an in-group.
- Shapes only outside the two lines indicate your casual friends. Are all your shapes similar?
- If you make the two lines into a single line you could be very reserved or self-centred.
- A coffin or a box means you are lonely and moody.
- Criss-crossing or x's inside the lines indicate a person who is only interested in close lasting relationships.
- Girls who make parallel lines are romantic, have mostly male friends. Men who make circular shapes have mostly girl friends.

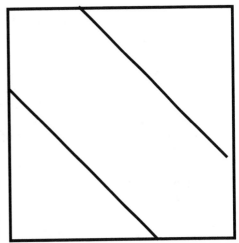

The box that reveals your Aspiration

- An arrow headed for the target shows an ability to work for a specific goal.
- If you make other lines or arrows pointing to the target, you're ambitious but faced with a choice of goals.
- If you obscure the symbol by turning it into something else, like a bird, wagon, lollipop, you are scatty, rebellious and imaginative.

Look back at your drawings on what inspires you the most. This might help you in your awakening process.

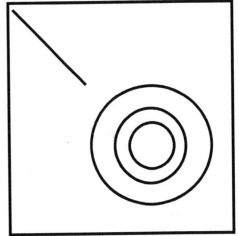

The box that reveals how Disciplined you are.

- If you accept the symbol and make a geometric design by duplicating the square, you are able to accept discipline and work with other people in an organisation.
- If you fight the black square and make a curved irregular design, you are stubborn. Either a trouble maker or a potential genius, or both.
- If you make some squares and some round shapes you're confused and should start a new romance, get a new something.
- If you create a three dimensional doodle you have a multidimensional insight to various obstacles or opportunities.

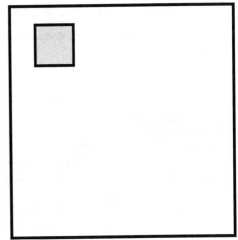

This box reveals how you think about Sex

- If you have used this symbol as a solid shape (like a building or a barber's pole or a animals neck) it shows a healthy uninhibited attitude towards sex.
- If you leave the space between the lines blank and obscure the symbol, if shows you're modest, shy but generally nervous about sex.
- A tree indicates an identification of sex with marriage, home and children.
- If there is fruit on the tree, this person is extremely keen on children.
- If it is a rocket-------well!

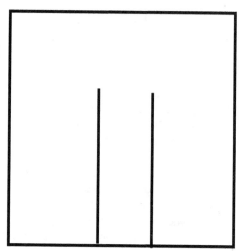

This box reveals your level of Confidence.

- If you have drawn above the line you are well-adjusted.
- If you draw a ship that is moving , you are very secure in yourself.
- If you have only drawn below the line you don't have all that much trust in yourself.
- If you drawn above and below the line, which part of your drawing is the most important?
- If you draw someone drowning, you're worried about the future.
- If you make a chain or a pattern out of the centre line then you are hard-working and hardly ever make a mistake
- If you create a three dimensional drawing you have absolute faith in the power of the human .

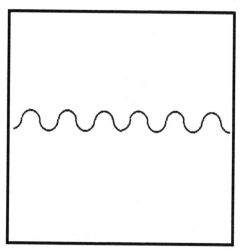

This box reveals how Competitive you are.

- If you play noughts and crosses in this square you are competitive.
- If you draw a winning game you are a winner, or at least aggressive.
- If you make a winning game by cheating you're tricky and probably rich.
- Men usually win with x's women with circles.
- If you obscure the symbol and don't play nought and crosses, you're passive and uncompetitive.
- Girls often make a box or a home symbol showing 'wifely' qualities.
- Some people will play the game using their own symbols. These people secretly wish to conform to others.

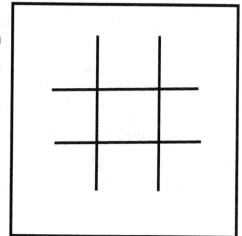

This box reveals if you have an imagination.

The dots in the box are often a challenge for people.
- If you use the dots as part of a specific picture it shows you are imaginative.
- If you secure the box by drawing a solid circle around or through them, you're practical, pragmatic, logical.
- If you created a drawing and wiped the dots away you are very willful.
- If you do nothing in this square you are unimaginative and will lend people money to be creative for you.

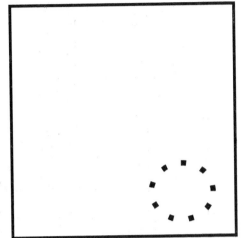

This box reveals if you have reached maturity.

- If you close these circles you want to be protected and still need approval.
- How tightly did you close them?
- If it was very closed you are still influenced by what you learnt as a child.
- If you don't close the circle you are independent and your ambitions and you can vision your future.
- If you make an ear-you have a secret.
- If you made a cup you have a loving maternal or paternal disposition.

This box I found so far the most revealing of all of them. It's amazing how many people still close the circle.

This last box reveals how social adaptable you are.

- If you go along with this symbol and echo its shape like a moon, face or a sun-rise it shows ability to get on with various types of people socially. You have good manners and you get on with people.
- If you fight the symbol and make ugly or squarish shapes, you don't mix well at parties.
- If you chop or reshape the symbol you are possessive in relationships

There is a lot more to be said about doodling. You will find that every time you doodle while you are talking over the phone, or you do this exercise again at a later stage, you will doodle totally differently.
I will share with you what I have found to be an often accurate interpretation, when people doodle in depth.

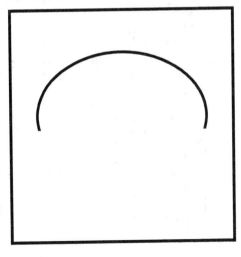

214 The Language of Light

Your Doodles in Depth

Occasionally someone will zip through the doodling exercises making scrawls at random and not really getting down to it. I know that these people are not yet ready to do any self reaching. I rarely had people in my courses that were not interested unless they were dragged to my classes by a friend.

Very random drawings often revealed that these people were generally very shy, kindhearted but ashamed of their own drawings.

- Ask yourself, are there many (if any) human figures in your 12 squares? A person who draws figures identifies with people, makes friends easily and is sociable.
- If you used words or write into the pictures you are an intellectual and can think abstractly.
- Some people who write often in their mind-drawings like to attract attention to themselves.
- If you have drawn outside of the 12 boxes it shows that you have a rebellious nature.
- If your drawings show a perspective, it indicates that you are a person that can plan ahead and carry ideas right through the five stages.
- People who draw in perspective are often employers instead of employees.
- Lines that reflect a horizon in doodle drawings are often done by people who look before they leap and then look again. They also don't get involved all that easily.
- Grotesque, frightening faces (monsters, pirates, skeletons) are often done by people who are unsociable. Those people only get on with others on their terms.
- Drawings of food indicates a person that feels unappreciated and want to be rewarded, complemented and taken care of.
- People who draw food could also indicate that they are hungry.
- Shading in any of the drawings indicate a sensual nature. There people are loving and kind.
- A fish in any of the boxes is often the symbol of wisdom. How is it used?
- Eyes, ears and a mouth in drawings often reflect a suspicious nature. These people always read the small print. They like to own their own property
- People who draw clothing, jewellery and anything that has an a external appearance take great care of their public image.

Interpretations

The Numbers with their vibrational Influences in your drawings.

The energy pockets that are embedded in our energy field all vibrate on different wavelengths. The following chart has been useful to me when I studied the art-analogue symbolism drawings of my students.

THE NUMBER **1**
- The key colour is Red.(beginnings)
- The energy of; Passion, Determination, Danger and Courage, Obsession.
- The tonal vibration letters are; I A S
- The gemstone is; ruby.
- The positive vibes are; Determination: Leadership, Individuality and Courage.
- The negative vibes are; Selfishness, Stagnation, Arrogance, Indecision.

THE NUMBER **2**
- The key colour is Orange.(cooperate)
- The energy of ; Warm energy, Motivation, Good and Faith.
- The tonal vibration letters are; T B K
- The gemstone is; moonstone.
- The positive vibes are; Cooperation, Receptiveness, Diplomacy, Consideration.
- The negative vibes are; Self-pity, Aggression, introversion, Pettiness.

THE NUMBER **3**
- The key colour is Yellow.(enjoyment)
- The energy of; Peace, Intelligence, Wisdom, Celebration and Spiritual knowing.
- The tonal vibration letters are; C U L
- The gemstone is topaz.
- The positive vibes are; Cooperation, Receptiveness, Diplomacy, Consideration.
- The negative vibes are; Self-pity, Aggression, introversion, Pettiness.

THE NUMBER **4**
- The key colour is Green.(practical)
- The energy of abundance, growth, vitality, and aspirations. The tonal vibration letters are;V M D
- The gemstone is emerald/ jade
- The positive vibes are: Cooperation, Receptiveness, Diplomacy, Consideration.
- The negative vibes are: Self-pity, Aggression, Introversion, Pettiness.

THE NUMBER 5
- The key colour is BLUE. (change)
- The energy of; healing, wholeness, renewal and balance. The tonal vibration letters are; V M D
- The gemstone is turquoise/aquamarine.
- The positive vibes are; Freedom, Travel, Resourcefulness and Versatility
- The negative vibes are; Self-indulgence, Unpredictability, Discontent and Irresponsibility.

THE NUMBER 6
- The key colour is INDIGO (responsibility)
- The energy of; alertness, well being, perception, healing prosperity. The tonal vibration letters are; X F O
- The gemstone is pearl/sapphire, lapis.
- The positive vibes are; Balance, Consciousness Service, Education.
- The negative vibes are; Chaos, Self-righteousness, Interference, Obstinacy.

THE NUMBER 7 (faith)
- The key colour is PURPLE
- The energy of; Distinguished, Respected, Proud, Enduring.
- The tonal vibration letters are; Y P G
- The gemstone is amethyst
- The positive vibes are; Inner wisdom, Philosophy, Intellect, Spirit.
- The negative vibes are; Ignorance, Aloofness, Sarcasm, Skepticism and Pessimism

THE NUMBER 8
- The key colour is BROWN/PINK (achievement)
- The energy of; loving, nurturing, Compassionate, Flexible, Tender, Faithful, Trusting
- The tonal vibration letters are; O Z H
- The gemstone is diamond
- The positive vibes are: Executive power, Success and ability, Good judgment, Material freedom
- The negative vibes are: Greed, Abuse of power, Vindictiveness, excessive ambition.

THE NUMBER 9
- The key colour is GOLD/ALL PASTELS (completion)
- The energy of; Treasured, Illuminated, Glowing, Sunshine.
- The tonal vibration letters are; I R
- The gemstone is opal/gold
- The positive vibes are: Universality, Completion, Accomplishment, Compassion.
- The negative vibes are: Impracticality, Wastefulness, Bitterness, Pickyness and Wickedness.

Interpretations

THE NUMBER 11
- The key colour is BLACK/WITH OR PEARL GREY (intuition)
- The energy of; Purity, Chastity, Integrity, Clean, Idealistic.
- The element is silver
- The positive vibes are; Spiritual revelation, Idealism, Emotionalism, Future vision.
- The negative vibes are; Lack of development, Futility, Imperiousness, Depression.

THE NUMBER 22
- The key colour is; CORAL/RUSSET (greatness)
- The energy of; quit energy, reassuring, open, stimulating.
- The element is; coral/copper red gold
- The positive vibes are; Master extrovert, Power on both planes, Financial stability, Complete control.
- The negative vibes are; Destructiveness, Exploitation, Bankruptcy,

THE NUMBER 33
- The key colour is; Sky Blue (inner wisdom)
- The energy of; The attainment of wisdom, Rebirth.
- The element is; lapis lazuli
- The positive vibes are; Master teacher, Worldly success, Skill and fame, Perfect relationship.
- The negative vibes are; Oppression, Poverty, Misuse of power, Devastating relationships.

Use this vibrational chart to evaluate your exercises on THE COLOUR AND OUR SENSES and the SOUND OF YOUR NAME.

When we are evaluating our exercises you have to take into consideration that as we progress on our journey to reach full consciousness, the responsibility that goes with it is enormous.

The more aware we become the greater the fall back into darkness so to speak. Our Divine supreme Creator. All that IS, is both polarities. There cannot be one without the other. There would be no yardstick to measure or know any balance in creation.

There is no <u>judgement</u> on energy, just an observation.

We humans use the term of good and bad but that perception completely vanishes as we awaken. We will always keep making an <u>assessment</u> on situations and make choices as to which polarity we will follow, but we never make a judgments anymore. Our soul awareness that is awakening through our biological consciousness(our physical body) does not perceive at all. It just experiences.

Your body symptoms on the Second level of awakening.

On the second level of our awakening major changes are happening in the brain and its chemistry surrounding the electromagnetic energies. Annelies told me that the symptoms are often headaches, blurry vision, loss of hearing and sometimes chest pains. Chest pains are due to the expanding energies of the heart as it opens to deeper levels. Vision and hearing are being realigned to function differently. The mental body begins to wonder if it really is in charge and individuals get strong inexplicable and undeniable urges to follow spirit without hesitation. Individuals may get flashes of telepathy, clairvoyance and nearly all begin to experience empathy. This is a time of feeling, of honouring and accepting and validating the emotional body and learning to control it.

Telepathy

Our Psychic hearing centres are:

The Second Sacral Chakra and Fifth Throat Chakra.

On this awareness level we realize the habitual nature of thinking and behaviour and we get to look at de-programming and re-programming from our interaction with parents, peers and society etc. Our lower mental body decides to tune to spirit, dreams change and may become more 'lucid', you get feelings of dé ja vu. Ingrid in her journal shared this second level in great detail in **The Awakening Clan**.

Our thought processes become non linear. Often at this stage we oscillate between knowing and doubt. Change seems to be constant and we consciously begin to discern from our heart rather than judge from our head that is used to 'conditioned responses'.

In order to awaken to this level our Sacral chakra has to be in harmony with our Throat chakra. This means we have to speak our truth. Especially when it comes to sexual matters.

We have to come to terms with any sexual distortions that might even have been inherited from our parents. If we have chosen to experience sexually abusive relationships, believe me it was a wake up call from Spirit, if the soul has chosen to ascend from this illusion. The body symptoms above are worse because the body avatar is struggling. Start a dream journal if you have not already done so.

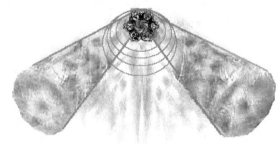

What we utter, say or voice to others often comes from both these centre of awareness levels.

Our ability to communicate on multidimensional levels makes us the co-creaters we are.

Some people are more direct in their approach and some are what we call 'diplomatic' and like to dress their words up with sugar coatings as not to be hurtful, or they are not sure themselves but have the need to say something.

For whatever reason we have the need or necessity to communicate, our energy field interacts with others from the awareness level we hold in both these chakra channels through our body language.

Our emotional expressions

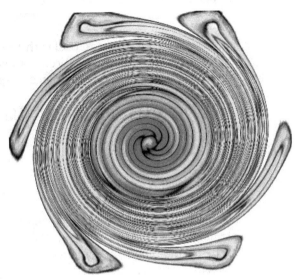

The two mandala exercises prepared us for the amazing revelation that we communicate through colour, line and shape as well as with words.

Throughout this workbook we deal with the three ways through which we interact with our reality.
- Our Body Language
- Our spoken or written (typed) word
- Our art-analogue mind-drawings.

Those three ways of reflecting our reality keeps it there!

As we study the emotional expressions on the mandala on the right you will find that the expression of anger (on the top middle) is bright red and fear is solid black. Meaning that the feelings of Anger are coming up from the Base Chakra

Tranquillity and joy is expressed through the Sacral chakra, being Orange, but feelings of guilt are also expressed in Orange. The sun symbol is also Orange. Orange is also used in the middle of the symbol of the flag.

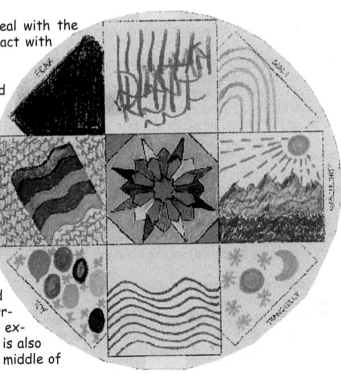

The Orange and Blue energy in Your drawings

Orange in drawings often seems to deal with the feelings we have towards ego striving. If emotional expressions and feelings are drawn out with the colour orange, it often reveals that the thoughts on this wavelength are a reflection of a great self-esteem, ambition and the like.

The gift of inner power
Level Two

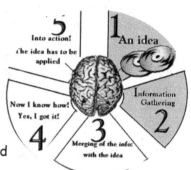

This secondary Scarlet ray's quality <u>activates the sexual/creative spirit</u> in humankind

- The archetype from the tarot deck, the Lovers,
- The astrological personality type of Scorpio/Libra,
- The energy of the Moon, all guide us to balance our left and right thinking mode hemispheres.

The Orange/Scarlet Chakra (your sensation centre)

DEEP ORANGE is often associated with feelings surrounding autumn.
Again a <u>lot of Pink</u> in a drawing often reflects some immaturity or naivety in the person. <u>Or clear, bright pink</u> speaks of human affection that has been softened by sorrow.
PALE ORANGE in a drawing can also be how we express the beauty of things or experiences.
Some people will use Orange instead of red as a colour that expresses to them having confidence, or believing in themselves or something they are not afraid of. It all depends on the drawing exercise.
  THE LACK OF ORANGE in a drawing can suggest what we need to embrace ourselves with in order to feel alright within ourselves; to love ourselves. Some relate to the feeling of entropy (tendency to decay) so they will not use orange in their drawings.
  Orange can sometimes reflect a feeling of boundaries in one's life.
  When our energy is blocked in this chakra, we are likely to be driven by our ambitions to the point that it separates us from others.

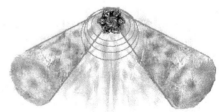

The Hidden symbols in Orange

The Illusion of our Time

CIRCLES in drawings
- The circle is widely accepted as a symbol for eternity, but with the Orange circle the meaning is often only known by the individual. The illusion of Time is associated with this symbol. It means the beginning of something.

A solid orange round ball or balls in a drawing can contain lots of emotions that result from intimate sexual hurts.

CROSSES,
- Crosses, lines or strong marks in orange also sometimes just reflect a hostile attitude towards authority. Depending on the drawing exercise, any crosses mean hidden feelings that are stirred to do with our sense of identity.

ARROWS.
- Any orange arrows in drawings means you must look at what they are pointing .

A CROSS
- Crosses in general can also symbolise a state of mind. It can mark a special place, or it can mean the person is dealing with life's difficulties and is at a crossroads to do with addictions to sensations.

DOTS.
- Dots or stipples in Orange could demonstrate an awakening to the value of true wisdom.

HEARTS
- Orange hearts in drawings again are mostly symbols of love, however, the orange heart may also represent spiritual fervour.

SQUARES
- Any boxes or squares in drawings gives the impression of firmness but they are rarely drawn in Orange.

TRIANGLES
- A triangle facing down stands for feminine and facing up masculine.

SPIRALS
- Spirals in Orange often express a longing for enlightenment. Orange spirals can also reflect an intimate relationship with someone.

THE INFINITE SIGN
- Orange Infinite signs in a drawing, especially when it's scarlet orange, symbolize an intimate time in a relationship experience.

222 The Language of Light

Your psychic hearing

- Take the section numbers where you used orange from your perception exercise on page .... and add them together. Root them down to a single digit number.
- Look up on your doodle interpretation pages and find out with which issue you used the colour Orange.
- See which quality vibe (if any) you gathered from that exercise and study the colours you choose for those numbers. Take your two Quality vibe numbers and write them inside the smaller circles.
- Get a general feeling about your energy field and read up about number vibrations with their attributes.

Any number that has the number 2 reflects your sexual force and above mentioned archetype of the Lovers.

Bring in the power of Structure with the sound of **I** as in **ice**. This will stimulate our sexual/creative force needed in order to feel good about ourselves. This will stimulate our secondary life force and activates our innate love of our fellow man. Through our inventions and expressions in art we heal our connection to others.

The gift of this energy level gives "structure to life."

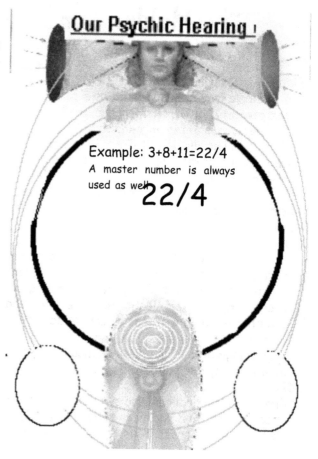

Example: 3+8+11=22/4
A master number is always used as well **22/4**

Here are some of the different Language of light symbols people drew.

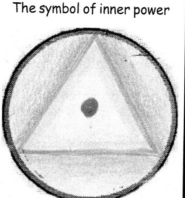

Symbol of Forgiveness

The symbol of inner power

Strength in foundation

The Blue energy in your drawings

This is the chakra that 'when damaged' people tell untruths or they have a fear that being honest to themselves will hurt others, so they rather hurt themselves by not telling the truth. People who cannot express or communicate to others shut themselves off. Lack of abundance is then often triggered by the personality aspect that is locked in the Sacral Chakra's needs for feelings of being secure and in control. Most of us have hidden anguish on different issues that can block our true abundance.

This Blue ray quality radiates outward from us when we connect through our communication skills.
- The archetype from the tarot deck is The Chariot,
- The astrological personality type of Cancer/Scorpio reflects an energy that can be both reflective and receptive.
- The energy of Neptune influences our persona.
- The elements of Water with Spirit guide us to balance our left and Right thinking mode hemispheres.

The Blue Throat chakra (your abundance centre)

THE COLOUR BLUE in drawings often seems to deal with communication issues. Blue in a drawing can suggest calmness, serenity and peace. Our brain's electrical response to blue seems to bring relaxation.
A LOT OF BLUE in a drawing often reflects that the person is ready to expand in height and depth.
DARK BLUE in drawings can be from the subconscious, like looking into a deep pool of water.
When drawings are MURKY BLUE, or colours like dark purple and even dark shades of green appear in drawings, that person's personality is in control during the drawing exercise due to the colour red that has blended in from the Base Chakra. Some people will use a symbol for water. Water cleanses, nourishes and cools our emotions. Sometimes a great deal of Blue is the colour of thought.
   Blue is the energy vortex that stimulates our awakening to our intuition. To some people the colour blue, especially dark shades of blue are feelings of depression, loss, or confusion. Each ray or light has specific qualities which refers, metaphysically speaking, to attributes to the specific manifestation patterns of that energy.
Blue involves a psychological rebirth.

The Hidden Symbols in Blue

CIRCLES in our drawings
- The circle is widely accepted as a symbol for eternity, but with the Blue circle the meaning is also often seen as the symbol of the expansion.
- A solid Blue round ball or balls in a drawing can contain lots of feelings that are related to the person's ability to communicate. Could it be a block? Or it could mean that doors will open.

CROSSES in drawings
- Any uneven crosses, lines or strong marks in Blue often reflect emotional feelings, depending on the drawing exercise. If there are any colours like browns, dark or murky green then those crosses mean hidden feelings that are stirred to do with our sense of taste that triggers memories from our childhood. A Blue cross in general reveals that the person is in deep thought.

ARROWS in drawings
- Any Blue arrows in drawings point to new inspirations to do with marketing and promotions. Reaching upward means they are pointing towards a higher dimension of awareness. When they go down look to what colours they are pointing.

HEARTS in drawings
- Blue hearts are often drawn by people who are in professions that deal with communication skills.

SQUARES
- Squares give the impression of firmness and are often related to things of our material world, but they are rarely drawn Blue unless they represent the voice within. Light and dark blues all vibrate according to the persons state of awareness. Dark Blue can also be a negative reaction to something. It can symbolize a dark deep pool without a bottom.

SPIRALS
- Spirals in Blue are often drawn unconsciously. They can mean that the person is searching in the deepest recesses of his/her unconscious.

AN INFINITE SIGN
- An infinity sign in a drawing, especially when it is in Blue, symbolizes communication links with the unknown.

SWIRLING LINES
- Swirling lines of blue activate the free flow of expressive energies within us. When colours of red and green are added, finality is added which creates a balance. Blue is the colour that in man trigger inspirations for an abundant life.

LOTS OF BLUE in a drawing can reveal that a person that has been suppressed in childhood escaped into their own fantasy world while drawing.

Interpretations 225

For many the colour Blue reflects a devotion for one's soul purpose.

Different colours of Blue in the drawings are often the colour that is used to express the real self when communication skills have not yet been developed.

Because of the connection with the Sacral Chakra the vibration of Red/Orange is blended with the Blue vibration. Colours like dark purple, dark shades of green or brown shades reveal issues from our physical body.

The shapes in our drawing where Blue is most prominent can reflect that your Throat vortex is activated through the sense of taste but it will be healed by the power of our voice.

Take a deep breath and bring in feelings of freedom from the known with the sound of **O** as in boat.

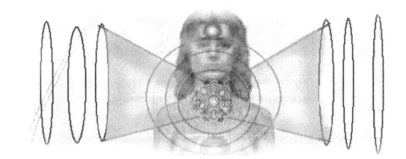

This will stimulate our Throat chakra and strengthen our ability to communicate with our fellow man.

Our self image is very challenged on this second level of awakening. Our soul has for the first time discovered what the experience really is like to awaken through a human body. Our egos first feel threatened by this powerful force, but gradually our personas are attracted by the love and wisdom of the energy force from the soul. Slowly our personalities allow more of soul power to share in our daily activities.

The geometric shapes that articulate all the spaces and relationships, patterns and proportions, which are the building blocks of our universe seem to affect or influence our perceptions. Plato expressed them as Solids that makes up our world of physical matter.

On the following pages I've created a chart that guides you in your interpretations of your mind-drawings.

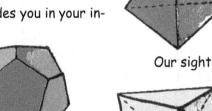
Our sight

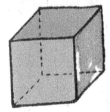
The sense of smell

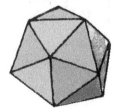
The sense of taste

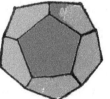
The sense of smell.

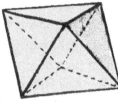
Our hearing

The mind-drawing formats in this workbook also connect with the 5 senses of seeing, hearing, tasting, smelling, touching and sensing energy.

226 The Language of Light

Your Body Language

The 9 masks we wear

2

2 THE STAR
The face, expression in the form of a symbol or feeling drawing in the star represent your personality's characteristic. This drawing is the reflection of how you see and feel about yourself.

1

As you go back to your exercise on the COLOUR OF YOUR SENSES, you were asked to choose three shapes from the eight platonic solids and number them in preference 1-2-3

Your <u>first choice</u> of any of the eight formats. That number would be the interpretation of your star. Your second and third choice would be any of the other seven format's interpretations.

3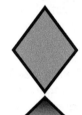

1 THE PENTAGON (down)
Which face do you show to your close family? This can be a partner, a very close boyfriend or girlfriend, parents, brothers or sisters or your children (if any). You feel very close to them and they don't run away if you feel down, sad or even angry.

4

3 THE DIAMOND
Which face do you show to an intimate friend? This is usually an intimate partner, husband, lover or someone you have a special relationship with.

5

4 THE PENTAGON (up)
Which face do you show to your colleagues? People you either work with or spent a lot of time with. This can also be a neighbour or customer.

6

5 THE SQUARE
Which face do you show to your good friends? You like their company and you are on a similar wavelength. You call on them if you need to talk.

6 THE CIRCLE
Which face do you show to your relatives? These people are not close, some are even strangers, some are people you just tolerate because they are family ,but they are not your choice of company.

7

7 TRIANGLE (up)
Which face do you show to authority? Do I need to say more!

8

8 THE HEXAHEDRON
Which face do you show to your acquaintances?

9 TRIANGLE (down) which face do you show to a beggar, hobo or a persistent salesman.

9

Interpretations 227

Your **First** choice
What mask did you wear?

You express a well grounded sense of identity. You show a sense of self-worth and follow your soul purpose.

Your faces show that you apply your spirituality in a grounded way, but you are not always sure that you will achieve your vision

Your face shows a joyful and ebullient inner spirit but learn to listen to your inner self and trust your basic instincts.

Your face is open, showing a kind, friendly and often mature warm compassion. You work well as a nurse.

You are in balance but your face does show that you are still very overcautious. You have an affinity for neatness.

Your face shows a joyful and ebullient energy but you can be tired through overactivity. Learn to be still and listen.

You are gentle, reliable and can make people secure but you withdraw away from others and become too self-absorbed.

You are an imaginative person full of fresh ideas. You are popular, express well and can deal with demanding situations. You are spiritually orientated.

Your **Second** choice
What mask did you wear?

You show that you know what you want. You have a determination to follow your ideas. Your soul is aware through your intent.

Your face shows that you find it a challenge to ask for acknowledgement when you give out orders to others.

The mask you wear hides your greatest challenge which is to make time for yourself and find the stillness within.

Your face does show that you have a challenge in giving and receiving because you tend to neglect your own needs.

Your mask hides emotional hurts, Your challenge is to express your emotions so you act out of unfulfilled needs.

You are an intellectual who needs to get in touch with your physical body in order to express your body language.

Your strength is your silence and knowingness but you must be more outgoing to avoid inertia and melancholy.

Learn to express through your body language the demands of others and give yourself time to cleanse your body, mind, and emotions to prevent illness.

Your **Third** choice
What mask did you wear?

Your inner self is urging for you to follow your heart's desire. Love yourself enough to trust that the changes will bring joy.

You are hiding your creativity and innate capacity for faith, intuition and wisdom behind your mask. Become the real you.

Your face shows that you may have inwardly withdrawn. Try to take more risks than usual. Be more courageous.

Let go of your mask and allow the gentle part of your nature to shine. You are a grandiose being.

Your mask hides a lot of guilt, Mix more with people in order to lift your spirits. Feel more valuable.

You need to expand your mind in order to bring optimism into your life. Take a long holiday in the sun.

Be more flexible with a practical attitude towards your daily life. Avoid escapism into meditations.

You love a welcome challenge that involves change if it has to do with transformation. Be prepared to go through turmoil and hurt.

Your body symptoms on the Third level of awakening.

Our Light body is gradually created due to the experience of shifting our observation points. Why I say this is because our current physical body, as it mutates and absorbs more Light on a cellular level, is unified during our resting periods in order to be realigned with our energy fields towards higher frequencies and higher octaves of Light. The following information describes the actual physical process and common symptoms as this change occurs on our third resurrection level.

During this level we draw people into our lives for mutual support and stimulation of growth. We question what is real daily and our mental process and how we identify with others and ourselves changes rapidly.

Re-evaluation towards our relationships, jobs, home environment and living styles is creating great upheavals due to our shifting perceptions, which urges us to let go and move on.

We change our friends, jobs, we relocate, everything feels to be in a state of flux but we feel lighter, vaster, freer somehow. On this level of awakening the Light quotient in our cellular organism is 33% - we feel as though we are opening up our inner senses.

On this level there is simply no room for denial. We begin to lose emotional attachments to others that are not on our awakening path.

Our psychic senses like clairvoyance, clairaudience etc. becomes natural to us. Our heart chakra opens more, we become more 'real' with other emotions, we just have to be ourselves! We gradually release more blocks and old patterns. During this level we are focussed with great intensity as we seek to rid ourselves of more emotional baggage. We feel more in tune with each moment, feeling very present and flowing with life.

Chest pains (angina) are more common as the heart continues to open its energy fields. Fear based thought forms at this level are released as our energy fields of all the subtle bodies are realigned through the heart. Pressure at the forehead or back of the head is due to the opening of the pituitary and pineal glands as they absorb more light. When these glands are fully open, activated and functioning at the highest level, ageing and death slows down until it stops altogether. When the pineal gland is fully open we experience life multi-dimensionally yet our world of duality seems to increase as we leave it behind.

Some days we feel connected and joyous and at other times we are in fear and caught up in survival issues. Dietary wise, we feel attracted to eat less or more light, live food.

Most people at this stage have ceased to eat meat. Some people begin to feel the effects of alcohol on their vibrational fields.

Your Violet/Indigo energy through your drawings.

This Sixth ray's quality radiates inwards. This centre when active will be watching life as a magic show from a beautiful place deep inside where everything is peaceful—all the time.

The gift of Clairvoyance.
Level three
The Third Eye chakra (your conscious awareness centre)

- The archetype from the tarot deck is Judgement.
- The astrological personality type of Capricorn/Pisces reflects an energy that can be both reflective and receptive.
- The energy of Saturn influences our persona.
- The elements of Earth and Air guide us to balance our left and Right thinking mode hemispheres.

Your Psychic intuitive centre

The colour VIOLET in drawings is often used with people who are searching for a spiritual experience.

INDIGO/VIOLET in a drawing can suggest that people are settled in their careers and in their beliefs. Our brain's electrical response to violet seems to open our pineal gland in order to receive those vibrations or wavelengths we call Indigo. Our pineal gland can be seen as our computer storage library of all that the soul has ever done.

A LOT OF VIOLET in a drawing often reflects that the person wants to expand in spiritual height and depth.

INDIGO in a drawing is also a sign of balance between the lower and the higher mental bodies. Some people will use lots of violet because they know it is a spiritual colour and they are preparing their personalities for a release in control. Sometimes a great deal of Violet in a drawing is a sign that the person has a strong intuitive knowledge about something and looks for a conformation. This person must follow their heart, not their head.

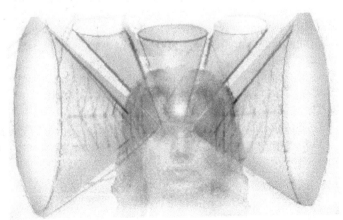

Your Hidden Symbols in Violet/Indigo

CIRCLES in our drawings
- The circle is widely accepted as a symbol for eternity, but with the Violet/Indigo circle the meaning is also often seen as the symbol of mental and spiritual expansion. A solid Violet round ball or balls in a drawing can contain lots of feelings that are related to the person's ability to intuitively access their akashic records.

CROSSES
- Any uneven crosses, lines or strong marks in Violet mixed with Orange becoming brown often reflect emotional feelings, depending on the drawing exercise. Any crosses mean hidden feelings that are stirred to do with our perception in connection with our sense of sight.

ARROWS
- Any Violet arrows in drawings point to new inspirations to do with mental activities. Reaching upwards means they are pointing towards a spiritual awareness. Reaching down can mean that an emotional obstacle is blocking the person.
- A Violet/indigo cross in general reveals that the person is very spiritually orientated.

HEARTS
- Purple/Violet and indigo hearts are often drawn by people who are in a profession that deals with metaphysical, healing and spiritual issues.

SQUARES.
- Squares give the impression of firmness and often relate to things of our material world, but they are rarely drawn Violet unless they represent the voice of the higher mind.

SPIRALS
- Spirals in Violet or purple are often drawn unconsciously, they can mean that the person is in a meditative state while drawing.

AN INFINITY SIGN
- An infinity sign in a drawing, especially when it is in Violet symbolizes communication links with the higher self, or it reflects spiritual ascension.

DARK VIOLET OR PURPLE can also be a negative reaction to something. Feelings that have been unexpressed are stirred.

SWIRLING LINES OF VIOLET.
- Indigo activates the flow of higher intelligence. For many the colour Violet reflects an awareness of one's soul purpose.

The Language of Colour

The three primary hues- Yellow, Red, and Blue- are the basic building blocks of our colour spectrum

Nearly everyone is interested in colour, yet most people have very little comprehensive knowledge about this subject. A colour may also mean something different each time you use it. The energy that any colour projects to us is to our conscious perception a platform from which we perceive, depth, width, height, and emotions. It's through our awareness of 'feeling' the colours in our drawing that we can shift our observation point over the threshold of our present awareness.

If you have an analytical nature you will benefit from the theory below as you study the colours that are appearing in your work.

Theoretically, all the colours we know are derived from the three primary hues of Yellow, Red and Blue. The seven colours of our chakra spectrum are also attuned to the seven tones of the musical scale.

- NOTE A Vibrates to the colour INDIGO
- NOTE B Vibrates to the colour VIOLET
- NOTE C Vibrates to the colour RED
- NOTE D Vibrates to the colour ORANGE
- NOTE E Vibrates to the colour YELLOW
- NOTE F Vibrates to the colour GREEN
- NOTE G Vibrates to the colour BLUE

This is a synchronising Sand Mandala representing the 'essence' of compassion that was constructed by four Tibetan monks in Durban during September 2002
They came from the Nechung monastery in Dharamsala, India

The motif of the circle appears very early in human history, the purpose of these designs is a mystery, but so many were created that they must have been very important. The Tibetan Mandala serves as a visual aid to meditation. Even Stonehenge is an earthly reflection of this celestial wheel.
Any Mandala format helps us draw on unconscious reservoirs of strength that make possible a reorientation to the external world.

232 The Language of Light

Colour has two divisions:

- WARM - COLD and LIGHT - DARK

Colour has movement:
- Warm colours approach the observer (it moves out from the centre and is field-oriented)
- Dark colours recede from the observer (they move towards the centre and are ego-centric.)

.Every Colour has three qualities:
- HUES is a colour's name (L-Mode attribute.)
- TONE is a colour's lightness or darkness. (R-Mode attribute.)
- INTENSITY refers to the brightness or brilliance of a colour.R-Mode attribute of strong intensity seems Vivid, while a Hue of low intensity appears Dull.
- The everyday word"colour"combines these three qualities.

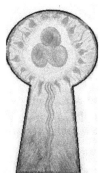

Soft pink , yellow and purple shows lots of compassion.

Western scientists are discovering that light might not just be symbolical but actually play a central role in all biological systems on our planet. Scientists have recently been able to see the beautiful, vibrating mandalic-like patterns of atoms and molecular structures that make up ever-changing forms of our phenomenal world.
The mandalas in this workbook help you to make a shift in your approach to your psyche—from linear (L-Mode) to circular thinking,(R-Mode) The language of the psyche (mandala) is a metaphoric or symbolic language.

The feelings many people seem to attach to a colour or black and white has influenced my interpretations over the years.

BLACK
- Black is the colour of darkness, evil, death, and mystery. It is associated with that which cannot be seen (beyond awareness)
- Our planet Saturn is associated with black, it stands for relentless unfolding of time.
- It is also associated with the understanding of death/rebirth.
- It may reflect feelings of depression, loss, or mourning.
- It may reveal the process of integrating our dark, shadowy aspects into our sense of who we are.
- Black chosen ahead of all others may suggest that you are unhappy with many aspects of your life and want to renounce everything.
- Most people like black least, expressing their desire to hold on to life, keep in control, and make improvements if they can.

WHITE
- White suggests purity, virginity, spirituality.
- At Christmas it signifies the purity of the Holy Child,the baby Jesus is also a reminder of the child that dwells in each of us. Look at a babies sleeping face and see the pure innocence we all once contained.

This very 'yang' drawing with lots of red done by a young man shows a will to survive.

- That part of us remembers the simple bliss of life before the separation of self and other.
- White sometimes represents silver.
- In Mandalas silver is related to the Moon.
- White can appear in different ways, it may be the white pigment applied to paper or the absence of colour which allows the white background to shine through.
- White can also reveal the loss of energy, or a challenge to your sense of who you are, or hidden areas of intense emotion.
- White can suggest clarity and readiness for change, heightens spirituality, opening to trans personal dimensions of the psyche that can be a source of inspiration, healing and enlightenment.
- White in Mandalas is a reminder of the light.

GREY
- Grey in a mind-drawing can symbolize depression, inertia, and indifference or lack of feeling.
- A lot of grey could mean that you may wish to conceal your true self from others and remain uninvolved with them and uncommited to their enterprises.
- Distaste for grey suggest the opposite, that you want to become involved with other people and you reject the option of staying aloof.

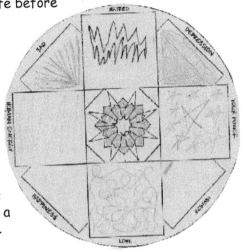

This above emotional expression exercise belonged to a very dear friend who passed away a few months after this mandala was drawn. The loss of energy is very obvious by the lack of red, the light pressure, and the amount of white in her mandala.

RED
- Red is the symbol for sacrifice, it has positive meanings that suggest the energy we need to survive, be healthy and transform ourselves to greater inner wisdom.
- Red can also mean the will to thrive.
- When red is mixed with another colour (purple, orange, or pink) it suggests that energy is present but strongly bound up with whatever is symbolized by the colour with which the red blended with.
- Red can also mean that you are committed to life, have the will to survive and the acceptance of the body fire of emotion.
- Making red your first choice indicates an urge towards success, intense experiences, and a full life.
- Rejecting red suggests that you already feel overstimulated and you are seeking to protect yourself from experiences likely to bring further excitement or aggravation.
- Reddish-brown indicates avarice, greed, selfishness.

DEEP DARK RED means sensuality.
SCARLET reveals an over-abundance of personal pride.
CARMINE- A CLEAR PURE RED-denotes strength, endurance and a high state of physical perfection.

A very grounded person's security drawing

234 The Language of Light

CLEAR, BRIGHT PINK bespeaks human affection that has been softened by sorrow.

BLUE

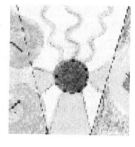

- Suggests calmness, serenity, and peace.
- According to Jung blue means height and depth. It also represents feminine attributes such as compassion, devotion, loyalty and unfailing love.
- Blue as a symbol for water suggests other meanings as well, water cleanses, nourishes and cools, water transforms substances by dissolving our connections with others.
- Blue is also associated with the function of thinking, the colour of thought. The colour blue is associated with Jupiter.
- Lots of blue mostly represents a need for tranquillity and contentment.
- If blue appeals the most they are expressing their need for peace, harmony, and an orderly environment.
- Placing little blue may mean that a need for harmony and mutual trust in relationships is not being met, or rejecting relationships because they are unsatisfying.
- Blue also denotes religious aspirations and devotion. If it has a faint touch of Lavender, the devotion is to a high and noble idea.
- Blue-grey denotes religious feelings motivated by fear. When blue is mixed with dark reddish-brown, the tendencies are narrow and bigoted.

YELLOW

- The colours on the Plus side are: Yellow, red-yellow (orange) yellow-red (minium, cinnabar) These colours excite, are quick, lively and aspiring.
- This is the colour nearest to the light. In its highest purity it always carries with it the nature of brightness, and has a serene, gay, softly exciting character. The eye is gladdened, the heart expanded and cheered, a glow seems at once to breathe towards us. Encourages detachment, suits mature minds.
- Yellow is the colour of the sunlight, warm and life giving.
- Yellow symbolizes the ability to grasp a pattern of meaning in a scatter of facts and impressions, it is also the symbol of intuition.
- Yellow could imply the need for release from conflict.

A preference for yellow may suggest that one is a person who presses forward into the future seeking ideas.

- Yellow in a mandala may represent gold. Gold suggests riches, or the wealth of the spirit.

The colours with their symbols in this art-analogue mind-drawing are truly an expression of inner pain, love, sorrow and regret, but the human Spirit of this friend is a strong one.

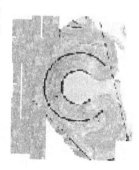

Interpretations 235

- A strong attraction to yellow suggests a desire for release from pressure and hope for greater happiness.
- Choosing yellow a lot shows a strong wish to escape from present difficulties.
- Using very little or no yellow indicates you may feel isolated from other people, disappointed in them, and suspicious of their intentions.
- Pure yellow indicates high intelligence and wisdom.

GREEN
- Green is the colour of nature.
- To Hildegard green expressed the presence of God in earthly matters.
- Green is associated with the planet Venus, to love beauty, to have confidence and faith.
- Green also reflects the ability to nurture and protect.
- Green is thought of as the symbol of Mother nature herself.
- Green represents the power to heal, and renew itself

A LOT OF GREEN compared to other colours indicates firmness, perseverance.
- Green can also mean a need to be recognized.
- NO GREEN at all may indicate that you may have been thwarted in your desire for recognition and you may feel beaten back by the failure of others to recognize your qualities.
- Green is the colour which typifies balance and rest.

PALE OLIVE-GREEN indicates sympathy and compassion.

GREENISH-GREY TONES reveal pessimism as pale grey indicates fear.

ORANGE
- Orange is the colour of the harvest moon pumpkins and autumn leaves.
- Orange in mandalas may suggest energetic striving, a strong sense of identity, and healthy assertiveness.
- It could also symbolize a wilful use of power, a hostile attitude toward authority, or no self-discipline.
- All clear, golden-orange hues bespeak an awakening to the value of true wisdom.

INDIGO
- Indigo in mind-drawings may reveal the awakening of intuition, the attainment

Thank goodness for the brilliant Green, Yellow and Orange colours in the mandala of a dear friend who had to experience such a great loss.

of wisdom and the development of a deeper and more meaningful philosophy of life.
- It also relates to the trying experience of the dark night of the soul: feelings of depression, loss or confusion.
- Indigo in mandalas can mean psychological rebirth
- Different colours of Violet or Indigo or purple in drawings is often the colour that is used to express the higher mind.

BROWN
- Brown colours express a feeling of being stuck between the impulse to go and the inhibition not to go.
- Brown may indicate the need for emotional security, a need for release from some situation which is bringing about a feeling of discomfort. It could reveal a low self esteem.
- Brown can indicate insecurity and a frustrated longing for greater physical comfort depending on the exercise.

NO BROWN AT ALL can also mean that you be suppressing your desire to enjoy physical sensations.

TURQUOISE
- This colour could mean that healing is necessary in order that you may get on with life or the need to distance oneself from painful events.
- It may indicate that the psyche is controlling the flow of memories which might be too painful.
- Turquoise in a mandala reveals often that the person has the tendency to resist emotions.

PURPLE-
- Purple is associated with royalty. Purple may also signify the process of personal growth
- It could also reveal an increased need for emotional support.

VIOLET
- Violet in a drawing means a vivid imagination, an ability to generate excitement, to attract attention. Large amounts in mandalas might reveal self-centredness, authoritarian or unrealistic behaviour.
- Choosing violet in your mandala suggests a wish to fascinate and charm others. It could indicate a degree of emotional immaturity.
- VIOLET is the energy vortex that stimulates clairvoyant skills. To some people the colour Violet, especially the purple shades trigger feelings of depression, loss or confusion. Metaphysically speaking, manifestation patterns of that energy involves a spiritual rebirth. To some people violet is the colour of death.
- Violet is the colour that in many trigger inspirations for a creative spiritual life but at the same time it can indicate a disappointment in relationships that reveals itself in an urge to hold back from serious commitments.

Awakening through the Etheric levels.

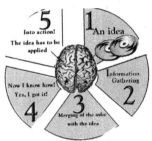

The Fourth level

The Fifth level

Your body symptoms through the Fourth level of awakening

Again you become much more aware of the vastness and multi-dimensionality of your nature, that you can be anything that you want to be, you cease to operate from obligation and relationships become transpersonal. You share words from your heart and soul and others may feel disorientated when dealing with you as they no longer have 'hooks' into you to link with. You operate from a deep level of serenity with heightened sensitivity and awareness yet feel grounded and transformed. We tend to disconnect from consensus reality and our choices and reality seem unreal to others.

As with the 2nd, and 3rd level, at this stage a strong re-evaluation starts to determine our income, our work and other people in our lives. As we begin the final surrender to Spirit the dissolution of the ego-self while ecstatic, can be most painful. Making the leap can be fearful even though we have evolved through eons of time to reach this point.

We may go back and forth, clinging to old comfort zones before completely letting go. There is no turning back and all must be released.

The fourth level triggers complete surrender and then ecstasy; the letting go of the "I". We realize that while free will is real it is also an illusion. It's there to guide us and to empower us to be One with Spirit. Survival fears leave. Though fears may surface, they seem unreal and are easily put aside.

During this awareness level our pineal and pituitary glands change shape. If headaches persist ask the Beings (your soul guides)who are working with you to simply 'tone it down' for they don't feel pain, or ask them to release endorphins (the brains natural opiate)

Our brain is being activated, particularly the cerebrum, the 'sleeping giant'. Cranial expansion is common; triangular 'seed crystals' in the brow and recorder crystals in the right side of the brain are activated along with the 8th, 9th and 10th chakras.

We begin to be hooked into the Languages of Light.
The pituitary and pineal glands are opened fully and work together to create the 'Arc of the Covenant', a rainbow light that arcs over the top of the head into the third eye that is a decoding mechanism for the higher dimensional languages.

You may find it hard to find words to express yourself as you may already start to think in geometries and tones.

When we start to become aware that nothing in our lives is meaningless, even the bad times, our lives will become enriched with new opportunities. When we embody the 10 first qualities of the Language of Light, our lives will be so full of joy, happiness, adventurous and blissful, we wonder how we ever survived without our Higher selves Love energy.

The Magenta/Violet energy through our drawings.

This centre is our gateway to cosmic intelligence. It only resonates with the highest purpose of our human existence. It has the potential of assessing full awareness.

The Gift of Freedom
Our psychic vision centre is:
The Crown chakra, our unity consciousness centre

Level four

- The archetype from the tarot deck is Justice.
- The astrological personality type of Pisces/Virgo reflects an energy that can both be reflective and receptive.
- The energy of Uranus inspires us to release any personality connections that are not in line with your ascension journey.
- The elements of Spirit and Water guide us to release our connections from our physical illusionary needs and replaces them with a total faith in the manifesting power of Spirit.

MAGENTA colours in drawings are always signs that there is a 'balance' in the person's observations.
INDIGO/VIOLET in a drawing can suggest that people are settled in their careers and in their beliefs, but if the colour red and blue is side by side you will know that their higher self is trying to send impulses that will open the pineal gland.

These colours together in drawings are an indication that the person is ready to receive knowledge from the higher realms.

A LOT OF VIOLET in a drawing often reflects that the person wants to expand in spiritual height and depth. If it is blended with red or blue so it becomes Magenta, the person is aware of their soul purpose.

MAGENTA in a drawing is also a sign of balance between the lower and the higher mental, emotional and physical/etheric bodies.

Some people will use lots of violet because they know it is a spiritual colour.

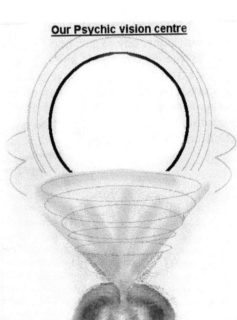

Our Psychic vision centre

240 The Language of Light

Sometimes a great deal of Magenta in a drawing is a sign that the person has a strong focus on their personal transformation. This person must still only follow their heart, not their head.

To some people the colour Magenta, especially if there are lots of shadings in purple and red, are trying to balance their emotional struggles.

LIGHT MAGENTA colourings looks like pink. This can also be a sign that a 'higher mind' is blending with the person. People who 'channel' often use pinky colourings in their drawings.

Pale colourings and shadings are often just an indication that the person is not very assertive in their dealings with life.

When the colouring in the drawings is very light with lots of white, this can again mean different things. The person can be low on energy due to illness (like my friends mandala on page 233) Or lots of uncertain situations are influencing the person's thinking modes.

Study your aura drawings.

The Language of Light symbols that you have drawn are starting to shift your 6th dimensional blueprint into a new template for your 5th dimensional Lightbody. Your body may change shape as the energy fields shift. You feel interconnected to all Being's everywhere and less connected to the opinions of others.

You release the desire for and the energy to sustain the 'game of separation and limitation' and feel truly free.

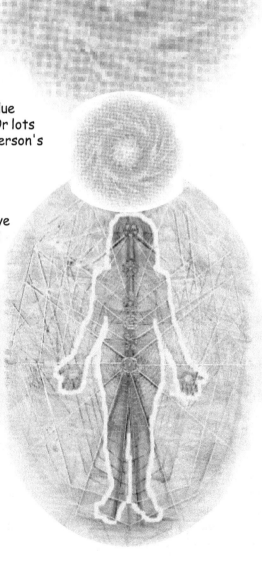

The Hidden Symbols of Magenta

CIRCLES in our drawings
- The circle is widely accepted as a symbol for eternity, but with the Magenta blend circle the meaning is also often seen as the symbol of being in the now. A solid Magenta round ball or balls in a drawing can contain lots of feelings that are related to the person's ability to be totally objective in their observations of life.

CROSSES
- Any uneven crosses, lines or strong marks in Magenta mixed with Blue are expressions of emotions that must be dealt with in a just manner. Any crosses mean hidden feelings that are stirred to do with our connection with our Higher Self. A Magenta cross in general reveals that the person is in contact with their Higher Self.

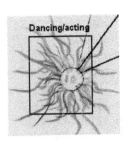

Action is associated with joy

HEARTS
- Magenta and purple or violet hearts are often drawn by people who are in a profession that deals with religions and spiritual issues.

SQUARES
- Squares give the impression of stubbornness and often related to things of our material world, but they are rarely drawn Magenta unless they represent the voice of the higher mind.

SPIRALS
- Spirals in Magenta are often drawn unconsciously, they can mean that the person is in a meditative state when the spirals are pale, but when they are of a strong colour their seventh chakra is active and the mind-drawing exercise becomes a creative expression of the Higher Self.

BIRDS, SWIRLING LINES AND WINGS.
- Any wings point to new inspirations to do with mental activities. When colours of red, with blue and purple are used they point to activities that take a lot of energy.
- Reaching upward means they are pointing towards a spiritual awareness.
- Reaching down can mean that an emotional obstacle is blocking the person.

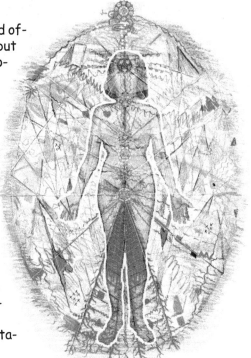

Your body symptoms during the Fifth level of Awakening.

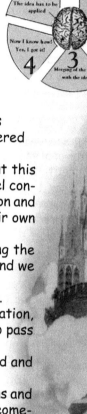

It was difficult to describe this level of awareness. It has to be done purely from a speculation level. Not many people have reached this conscious awareness level. Most of the information came from Annelies and POWAH.

On this level our perception point has so shifted, we tend to disconnect from consensus reality and our choices and reality seem unreal to others.

From the 4th and 5th level our inner light noticeably radiates out and by now we feel unbelievably grounded, connected, centered and filled with purpose and desiring only to serve.

For awhile we may still slip between the 3rd and 4th level but this settles down by the end of the 5th level. You then continually feel connected and operate purely from our Higher self level. Our intention and motivation is always for the highest, although others, due to their own inner triggers and issues may not always choose to see that.

During this 5th stage we begin to hook up to our I AM. During the last two levels we unify all energy fields, all chakras are unified and we become totally connected to our I AM.

We are one with Source consciousness and know all is possible.

DNA is no longer 2 strand but 12 strand and more; teleportation, manifestation etc. are instantaneous. Our light body allows you to pass through space, time and dimensions complete in our totality.

All levels of the lightbody have been constructed and activated and are connected to our physical body via 'spin points'.

These light matrix's lie along the physical acupuncture meridians and these lines of light form an intersecting network in beautiful geometries new 5th dimensional circulatory system of Light.

Cellular regeneration has been accomplished. Time is no longer linear but simultaneous. Past, present and future co-exist in parallels. There is no separation and we will fully manifest our vision of Heaven on Earth and express the ecstasy of Spirit.

In this 'frame' of conscious awareness many now access and create new types of Light based technologies, new community living, new systems of government and equitable food and resource distribution systems. All have received specialist training and skills to help create and manifest the New World - the 'Golden Age'.

"If we stop perceiving ourselves as egos, accepting instead that we are fields of energy, then we will change our view of reality, and our behaviour in it. As egos we need to defend ourselves. As fields of energy we are concerned about the appropriate use of energy, that is with impeccability."
Victor Sanchez, The Teachings of Don Carlos

Tieneke de Beer

Salute to the Sun

Through movement and sound we activate the seven major chakras

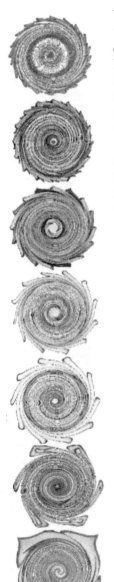

Every physical body has an individual sound. There are people who can hear the frequency and at what speed you are vibrating. It's the speed that rules your reality! Even in our world there are different realities. Some people choose to live in a war zone reality, which must be low, while others live in a tropical paradise. It's all irrelevant.

Each of your 7 chakras have their own wavelength and together they produce a resonance. This resonance determines the speed at which you are vibrating. (Love is experienced as high speed energy and hate and destruction as a low speed.)

Every cell within you body is a sound resonator that keeps you in shape through your muscular actions. These muscular actions (internal and external) create a sound, or wavelength that keeps your body visible within this 3rd dimension. When your body sound is out of tune you experience a dis-ease.

Through the use of sound from your vocal cords and the wonderful physical exercise The Salute to the Sun, we balance and strengthening the tuning of our bodies. We speed up our physical energy particles to super energy particles!

The sound vibrations of your physical body connects and resonates with the vibrations of atoms and molecules in and around you. There is no separation! Sound vibrations set air molecules in motion. Audible sound vibrations enter your ear, causing your eardrum to vibrate and send pulsations to every cell that is listening! You can feel sound vibrations through your body. If your soul has the intent to ascend, your soul will use your physical body as a tuning fork in order to ascend back to a 6th dimension reality.

The Booklet is used for your The Body Codes of Light

What to do with our cards?

We use them to become the builders of form, but this time we will assist in the changing of the vibratory rate of our world with its cosmic law on Cause and Effect

The Law of Karma

Cosmic Law and Man's law.

THE BIRTH OF OUR SOUL

Evolution follows Cosmic Law throughout every aspect of the great Cosmos. This Law is linked to the concept of consciousness. What is consciousness one asks? Can we call a computer a consciousness? It has a memory and many other aspects that almost resembles the workings of our brain.

For now I accept that everything around me is consciousness, be it inorganic or organic; meaning consciousness with or without a life force. All the solid matter around us is a form of consciousness. When I talk of beings or inorganic entities, I'm referring to soul particles that are broken away from an individual soul field. This separation came about when our 'creations' (Universes with their galaxies) dropped in speed/vibration. In order to rectify this imperfection, group souls divided into many oversouls. A further descent towards a 'reality' that is formed by matter, resulted in the appearance of individual souls.

Our 'soul' is like a library of accumulated consciousness that gathered experimental experiences of life, action and reaction. Our 'soul' imbues many embodiments and experiences 'life' through a persona (ego entities) in order to gather soul particles that have fragmented and fallen away from its primary soul library. Only on this lower dimension can we attract all our disunity thought-forms (fragmented soul particles) to ourselves and thereby take responsibility for our own distorted energy creations. (The law of Karma)

In the Sixth dimension, our soul realm, there is no longer an ego or personality attached to our soul. There is still You and Me but there is no sense of separation. Our Higher Self is the connection between the soul realm and the Physical 3D/4D realm.

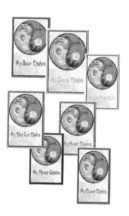

While the soul can merge with other souls, it remains a complete, unique reality unto itself. The Over-soul is the collective Soul Consciousness of individual souls. It dwells in the seventh dimension. This is where individual souls receive their plans for incarnation. Souls evaluate their progress in evolution on the seventh realm. Once a soul reaches a certain level of awareness (you the reader is one of them) he or she may begin consciously drawing experiences that maximize spiritual growth.

Ascension occurs when a soul evolves beyond the cycle of reincarnation and increases the vibratory frequency of the physical body sufficiently to graduate from the fourth to the fifth density level of evolution. This may mean that our body's cellular structure is speeded up to the point of becoming invisible to ordinary third dimensional consciousness.

The Creation of our World.

Through the builders of form

How did our 'dream' become the world of form? Annelies explained that all life on our planet is created from a etheric blueprint. This etheric blueprint is created by a supreme highly evolved intelligence. (God/goddess of all that is) It could be that we are these creators ourselves. Remember that I'm referring to the content of our <u>group soul's library</u>, that in turn divided into <u>oversouls</u> (sections within a library) who again separated into <u>individual souls</u>.(individual books) We humans are an expression of an individual soul. Like a book that has an author. Each individual soul is controlled by our spirit. (The primary essence of the divine)

As individuals we are only a part of the whole. The blueprint of every organic life form on our planet appears to be derived from a coded geometric building block known as platonic solids. They are in turn related to the five elemental energies we use in this workbook.

So now you know, our world is a programme — a virtual reality show. Ingrid's journal; **The Awakening Clan** is a virtual reality programme like ours.

Ingrid gives a lively account of her life and how she experiences the first two levels of awakening.

Part from the human evolution three other evolutionary intelligence were given the opportunity to develop and mature, but the evolution of each one of them differs radically from ours. They are the plant, animal and mineral kingdoms. Lately through a cohesive band of love, cooperation and unity work, we can ask for their assistance.

It's with the assistance the five elements of fire, water, earth, air and ether, and organic and in-organic beings that we again become the builders of form.

- It's through the element of fire that mighty Salamander beings will help you to transform any distorted disunity thought-forms.
- It's through the element of water that mighty Undine beings will help us purifying all our distorted emotional thought-forms.
- It's through the element of earth that the plant kingdom will come to our assistance whenever we ask for there help with grounding and staying in the moment.
- It's through the element of air that the mighty Sylphs with the help of the planetary beings will assist us to only speak of love and harmony with every breath we take.
- It's through the element of ether that the mighty angelic kingdom interacts with us. They will only help they are invited. If it is your intent to ascend this illusionary world then nothing is impossible to them. They will be your guides in times of need.

Through them we again learn to recreate and become once again the builders of form.

Your Chakra cards

Language of Light and Elemental cards

The activation of our Light body, the body of our Soul

The home is where the heart is, is a well known saying throughout the world. Why not build our <u>temple</u> from the idea of our homes. It's with this <u>body temple</u> that we can journey home. On this fifth awareness level we are using a format everyone can relate to in their own individual way. Most people live in a 'home' be it a flat, tent, boat, house, tree hut, igloo, rondavel...

Our homes consists of five major sections. 1 <u>Our environment around our home</u>. 2 <u>Entrance hall/reception/public place</u>, 3 <u>Kitchen/diningroom & Lounge</u>, 4 <u>Bedroom(s)</u> and <u>Bathroom(s)</u> Annelies suggested that you use these five sections through the three pathways as a platform to gather all your quality vibes in order to make a booklet. Later you will use this booklet with your cards for her ascension board game.

<u>My Language of Light cards</u>
Forgiveness:
  • My light fittings,
Structure:
  • Running of my household
Power:
  • Electricity /solar heating
Compassion:
  • The people in my home
Breath of life:
  • Flowers (fragrance)
Unconditional love:
  • Children, Pets
Freedom:
  • Transport

<u>My Seven chakra cards</u>
The Base Chakra card:
  • My entrance hall and kitchen
The Sacral and Solar Plexus card:
  • My Bedroom(s). Guest Room
The Heart and Throat Chakra card.
  • My lounge/dining room/patio
The Third Eye Chakra card:
  • My bathroom(s) (sauna, showers,)
The Crown chakra card:
  • My garden, view to the outside world, Our link with others. Garage.

<u>My Elemental cards</u>

My Earth card
  • My garden & pot plants
My Water card
  • For cooking and bathing.
My Fire card
  • For cooking & fire place
My Air card
  • My doors & windows
My Ether card
  • Music centre, telephone TV, PC, books, artwork.

Your dream Home example

I used a double story tree house with a view over the sea

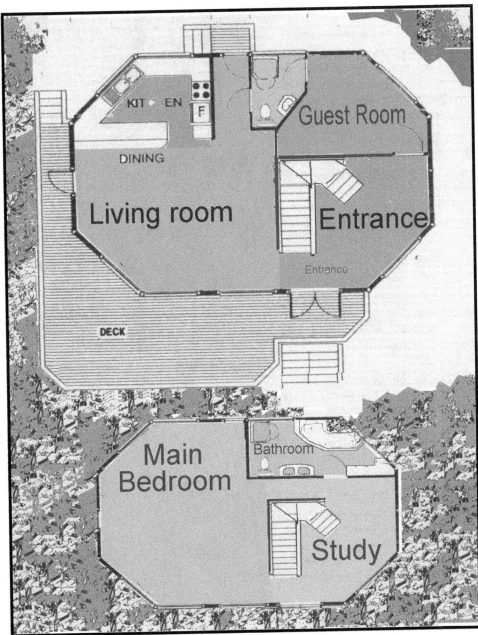

- You can make your own, or use this one and work out in which area of your house are you lacking any energy.
- Which section of your house has an abundance.
- It's in the activity of creating something in our minds that takes our attention away from our daily worldly affairs.
- Any creativity that grips your attention, if it gives you pleasure, it becomes a meditation.
- The thoughts we seed will shape our future manifestations.

Your booklet instructions - for the Awakening Game

My Base Chakra card
The <u>First level</u> of your awakening

This first consciousness centre is mainly preoccupied with food, shelter or whatever we associate with our personal security. The lesson in this vortex is to release the need to get 'enough' in order to feel secure.

My Sacral Chakra card
The <u>Second</u> level of your awakening

The sacral/sexual chakra represents our sensation centre. This vortex sits in front in the pelvic area and corresponds to the reproductive and urinary systems. It governs sexuality and emotions.

My Solar Plexus Chakra card
The <u>Third</u> level of your awakening

This centre is mainly preoccupied with power issues. The gift inherent within the third chakra is the right use of power, which is power based on unconditional love.

My Heart Chakra card

We have reached the fourth centre where 'work' is no longer performed unconsciously or mechanically. Our feeling nature is preparing us for a new energy flow which will increase our growth into higher consciousness.

My Throat Chakra card
The <u>Fourth</u> level of your awakening

This chakra influences our thyroid gland. This is our communication centre where the divine word is spoken through on the highest level from our higher self.

My <u>Third Eye</u> Chakra card

This sixth chakra which is associated with our inner wisdom rather than expressing outward into the world.

More information on the activity of becoming builders of form, you can find in Cyberspace.
www.ascensiontopics.com

My Crown Chakra card
The <u>Fifth</u> level of your awakening

This seventh energy vortex, which is an etheric chakra, is our highest spiritual channel. That means this vortex exist within the realm of the psyche; it's your channel to your Higher Self,

Booklet 251

Example of your chakra booklet section

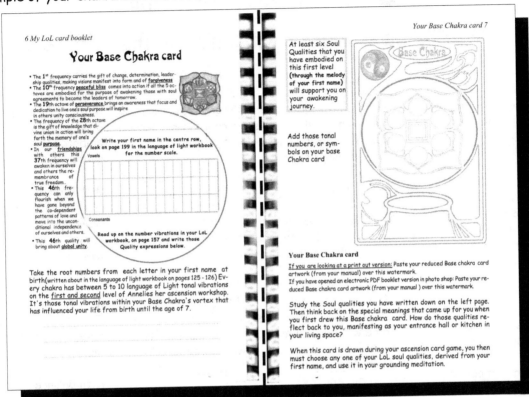

As your go over your mind-drawing exercises on each awareness level, you will have discovered how awake your soul consciousness is through your physical form. Who is in the driving seat. When you take that into consideration, ask yourself which quality of the Language of Light have you already embodied on a daily basis.

With that information you are going to build your dream house. This dwelling place can be anywhere. In the fifth level of awareness you can create anything you want. The Language of Light qualities that you have embodied determine how awake (aware) your soul is through the physical body. The more aware you become the more you are in control of your manifestations.

Each quality of the Language of Light represents an aspect that makes your home a divine temple others love to visit. A home from where you start to perceive all the energies around you that make up this illusionary world. A sacred space where all your experiences are expressed through the beauty and comfort of the objects around you. You are a reflection of the things in and around this Home.

A place where your loved ones enjoy a meal with you. A place where you can invite a master, a teacher, or a beloved. A place or temple that is completely created by the energy forces from your soul awareness.

You are this house. You are what is inside this house. You are all the aspects of this house or temple. And when the time has arrived that you are finished building your house with all its aspects, you are ready to play the ascension board game.

Build your Sacred Temple
With the Language of Light qualities you have embraced

With **Forgiveness** (Light fittings.) You will have the determination to pursue your soul purpose or your visions in order to manifest them into physical form.

—

With **Structure** (Household appliances) You will be helpful in maintaining a stable structure within your home.

—

With **Power** (Electricity or solar energy) With this inner power you can pursue your dreams.

—

With **Compassion** (The people in my home) All your family, friends and loved ones love visiting you

—

With a **Breath of life** (Flowers for my home) You will spread the fragrance of joy around your home.

—

With **Unconditional love** (Children or Pets) You will attract creatures of all kinds to your home.

—

With **Freedom** (A helicopter?) You can travel anywhere away from your home in style.

—

With **Direction** (Books) Your visitors, guests or companions will always know from which direction you view life.

—

With **Hope** (Fruit trees) You will always see an opportunity to enhance your environment.

—

With **Divine Union** (A soul partner) You could share this home with a soul mate.

—

With **Abundance** (Psychic energy) You will always have enough energy to manifest all your dreams.

—

With **Prosperity** (Your soul purpose or interests, hobbies) Your manifestations give others joy.

—

With **Unity** (Dining room furniture) I will always bring unity during mealtimes.

—

With **Perseverance.** (Relentless energy to build) I will always be there for myself and others.

With **Hidden Truth** .(A meditation corner in the garden) will guide you to awaken what was hidden before .

—

With **Consciousness** (technology like a TV or a PC) You will be stimulated through your interaction with others.

—

With **Peace** (Neighbours.) Your home is within a Loving community where everyone lives to their best potential.

—

With **External expressions.** (Letterbox and front door bell) Your resonance is inviting, people drop in.

—

With **Oneness** (Patio furniture) You will experience many conversations with others on your patio.

—

With **Function** (Crockery) Your home will host entertain and engage others through many parties and activities.

With **Magnitude.** (Unlimited possibilities with decor) You will expand your energy to embrace lots of adventures.

—

With **Purpose.** (Writing and painting or drawing tools) You will spend time being very creative in this home.

—

With **Integrity** (The mirrors in your home) they reflect your image of integrity.

—

With **Balance** (Hot and cold water) Everything in my home is in balance with my living conditions)

—

With **Dreams** Your bed is a vehicle from where you travel to multidimensional realms.

—

With **Action.** (A great sofa for the lounge) will activate all that are gathering in your home.

—

With **Illusion** (A fountain) for the hallway or lounge to spent creative moments at home.

More LoL Qualities with their attributes are published on our website: www.ascensiontopics.com

Example of your Language of Light booklet section

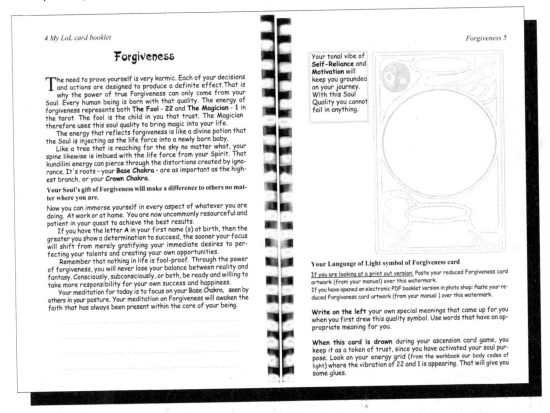

In order to plan, design, build and decorate a home, we need to know what we want in life. I discovered that when I was building my dream home in my sacred space, I could think of many illusionary objects that would make my home a place of beauty and tranquillity. All the objects around my home and garden in a way reflected the Language of Light qualities.

Through this method of building my dream home I discovered true abundance.
We are co-creators of our physical experience. Through the building of your home you are reminded that everything is possible. There is not lack of funds. You can choose any plot of land or place anywhere in the world. There are no obstacles you cannot overcome.

Creativity is often our fastest route to awaken our awareness. Through our creative body, mind, and spirit in action, we shift our perception. By our focus, our reality changes according to the level of psychic energy we hold in our field. This brings on a transformation on a deep cellular level. It will keep you young. Aging will gradually stop.

Choose the format from this workbook, or draw your own dream home, or join a group and together play with the cards from this workbook.

It will be your preparation for the ascension workshop on the decoding of your blueprint <u>first level</u> that Annelies has prepared for people who have the memory of heir ascension embedded in their DNA.

Are you one of them?

254 The Language of Light

Our ring bound A4 drawing manual

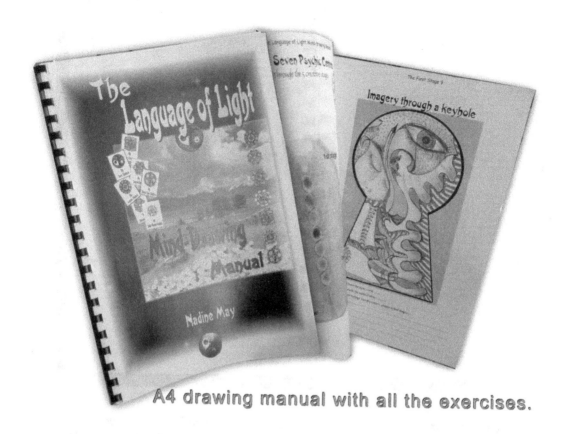

A4 drawing manual with all the exercises.

A work manual has been printed for students who would like to teach others; and for their students. This 141 page A4 manual is only obtainable form the below web site.
 I have included some extra Language of Light cards for people who work directly from the book.
 It is again with some regret that a coloured version of this workbook is not in print, but we felt that it was more important to make this workbook available(cost wise) for many.
 From October 2009 A full colour version, including a CD with both manual and the booklet can be obtained from:

www.ascension-workshop.co.za
www.ascensiontopics.com

Booklet 255

*The seven symbols that are found in your Language of Light elemental cards cards with your name and date of birth, this information is used for your further ascension journey with Annelies in her workbook: The Body Codes of Light. Published during 20 10

The elements of our world were created by the builders of form. We were once these builders of form. The fact that we have a human experience reveals that we have evolved through the seven major spheres (rays) to learn to be builders of form in order to become co-creators with the divine supreme Godhead. The seventh spheres (rays) hold within it's divine supreme force the etheric blueprint of our every manifestation.

Your are already a master.
You are already an ascended being.
You are already awake.
You are already all what you can be.
You are the dreamer.

Wake up!

Focus on one of the 48 personal symbols of your Language of Light Qualities, to be found in the pocket book below, for your daily meditation.

Meditations
on your
Language of Light Qualities

OUR SOUL QUALITIES, WE ALL HAVE WITHIN US, COME ALIVE THROUGH OUR MEDITATION!

Each Language of Light image is a vibrational key that reflects a soul quality particle of love. Each quality key that we invite into our living experience will have an effect on our daily lives. These keys can unlock distorted thought-forms that are locked in a frozen state within our mind field.
With each meditation on The Language of Light Qualities, more essence of our soul is embodied into our physical body.
These quality thought-particles of Forgiveness, Perseverance, Purpose, Friendship, Balance, Direction, Compassion, Unconditional love, to name a few, will have an healing effect on our emotional, mental and physical bodies.
It will activate our DNA /RNA

Index/Glossary

A

Akashic library 48
An etheric Auric field of a soul that manifests as a holographic medium on the seventh realm. It holds the cosmic history of each individual soul's every experience including possible off-planet experiences.

Akashic records 12,16
All creations that are manifested electromagnetically, through thoughts, emotions or actions and events of a soul are stored here.

Analogue drawings 15
Pictorial or symbolic images and shapes from the sub- and unconscious that can be translated.

Ancestral heritage 139
Biological genetic patterns and programming that are inherited through our parents, grandparents and forefathers.

Anthroposophical 194
System of philosophy founded by Rudolph Steiner

Ascension board game 155
This board game is played with 4 to 6 people. It's a holographic platform of a community where each individual uses their personal codes to gather psychic energy in order to ascend.

Ascension journey 144
An individual process of awakening consciously and transforming one's biological cellular vibration.

Ascension workshop 128
A 12 week genetic decoding workshop described in the novel: The Awakening Clan.

Assessment 219
An observation and accepting of values or a regard of something without having a judgment about it.

Auric field 138
An electromagnetic field that surrounds every organic being with a life force.(humans, plants, animals and minerals. This field contains information about that living entity.

Awareness levels 22
(1) A conscious knowing about one or more levels of realities. Different levels of an intelligence that has an ability to perceive the truth about a given reality.(2) An awareness of which chakra is involved in the physical, emotional and mental experience.

B

Base Chakra 27,38.68
(1) Also called the Root chakra. An energy vortex through which the soul experiences survival issues to do with the physical realm(2) A vortex that creates an etheric connection cord with planet earth.

Biological consciousness 155
(1) Our conscious awareness knowing on a physical cellular level. (2) Our physical body.

Bliss-bunnies 120
People who are into bliss without being grounded in reality. They are in total denial of their shadow and escape into a fantasy world of their own making.

Body avatar 43,168
The awareness of the nuclear spirit (life force) that holds the original blueprint of the full strands of RNA/DNA that originally manifested as the human specie.

Body of Light 12
A luminescent etheric 5th density mirror of our physical body that depicts a silicon crystalline structure.

Breath of life 250
A psychic quality of the soul that brings words of wisdom, love and truth into a physical experience.

C

Carbon based body 153
Any 3rd density life form that uses a carbon process to sustain a physical form.

Causal plane 162
(1) A realm where all thought-forms have created a sub-dimension whereby a soul can view future manifestations. (2) a crystal realm that controls the lower realms of creation.

Cause and effect, law of 130
What you sow you shall reap.

Characteristics 155
Certain energy particles that form patterns of behaviour emotionally, mentally and physically, which influences our perceptions of life in the 3rd Dimension

Clair audience 230

The ability to hear with the inner ear sounds beyond the range of normal hearing.

Clairvoyant 130
The ability to see with the third eye events or situations occurring in another physical location, dimension or density.

Colour therapy 194
he vibration of colour is used to harmonise the vibration of the physical body.

Consciousness 93
(1) The aspect of individual life forms within the divine creator that possesses the ability to be aware of itself.(2) The movement of intelligence.

Consonants 127
Letters that are not vowels.

Cosmic Awareness 142
A state of awareness whereby the individual perceives all of life's experiences as a reflection of the unified whole.

Crystalline body 153
Light body

D

Detachment 28
The act of removing any identification of the self with an emotion, event, thought or experience.

Distorted programs 13
Fragmented manifested creations.

Divine energy 145
Psychic energy, Soul energy. Essence emanating from the Godhead.

Divine Union 185
Where the feminine and the masculine gender within a soul merges in harmony, or when two individual souls live in harmony with each other in order to awaken their true potential.

Dodecahedron 157
A solid figure with twelve faces.

Dominant hand 180
The left or right hand that is always used for writing and drawing.

Dream journal 34
A notebook kept next to your bed.

Dysfunctional energy pockets 68
Distorted energy thought-forms that got stuck within our etheric grid structure.

E

Electric 153
Two opposite components that causes a electrostatic phenomena (excitement) through rubbing together. Male energy.

Electro-Magnetic 153
(1) Having both magnetic (female) and electric (male) energy properties. Both energy forces make up the ethers of the etheric plane.

Electromagnetism Law of 18
A harmonious attraction

Elemental 140
The powers of nature.

Elemental grid field 19
A crystalline web of light that is often seen around plants and trees in forests.

Elements 157
Substances that cannot be reduced by chemical means into simpler substances.

Emotional intelligence 161
A strong emotional intensity tempered by the sense to act appropriately when assessing a situation.

Energy distortions 154
Destructive thought forms.

Ether 156
A medium through which electromagnetic waves are transmitted into a higher frequency.

Etheric blueprint 16
A set of electromagnetic codes (program) that defines physical life forms through the RNA/DNA molecules.

F

Feng-Shui 42
(1) Chinese practices to create harmonious energy flows in a living area. Also used in designing buildings.

Fifth-dimensional 98
Starts with the etheric plane beyond the astral and mental levels where there is no more duality.

Free will, Law of 19
The ability to consciously choose how fast to evolve as a soul. The ability to decide how, where and when to experience a soul lesson.

Frequency 100
The rate (speed) of vibrations

Full consciousness 219
Supreme knowledge of universal laws.

G

Genetic blueprint 139
Multidimensional strands of RNA/DNA that holds the complex molecular proteins that formed the original program of humanoid life forms.

Genetic codes 160
DNA program through biochemical nucleic acids that constitutes the genes in all living organisms.

Genetic decoding 13
Genetic decoding formula through the creations of 22 divinity cards that hold the blueprint for the initiate that has the intent to ascend.

Genetic related karma 162
Karma that has been taken on by the soul through a specific incarnation. The parents carry a genetic pattern that will bring about a lesson for the incoming soul.

Geometric shapes 227
These are nonfigurative lines or shapes.

Geometry, science of 157
Numerology. The vibrations of numbers and their properties and relations of points, lines, surfaces, and solids.

God/goddess 129
Supreme highly evolved intelligence. The ultimate creator of all that is.

Graphology 198
Study of handwriting.

Group souls 249
A soul family that belongs to the same oversoul.

H

Harmonic overtones 125, 156
Sounds that are harmoniously produced by vibrating a sound in an exact fraction of its length.

Hexahedron 157
A solid figure with six faces. Female energy.

Hieroglyphs 14
Egyptian and other writings where the drawn object represents a word.

Higher astral realms 192
Soul planes from the 5th to the 6th density

Higher dimensional languages 240
The Language of Light

Higher mind 232
Higher intelligence our universal mind.

Higher Self 142, 154
Soul's true awareness. The aspect of the self that resides in the higher dimensions.

Hildegard von Bingen 206
A nun from the 12th century who wrote songs and sang them to glorify the almighty.(Those songs are still played today)

I

Icosahedron 157
A solid figure with twenty faces

Illuminati 82
A secret society of occult teachings from the Orions, Sirians, and the earlier Adamic races that became corrupted by power-hungry factions with the goal of total domination and control of the world and its resources. (See Maldek)

Illumination stage 28
Stage of enlightenment.

Illusion 13
A belief system or method of perception from a limited frame of reference.

Individual souls 249
Reality that is uniquely true to one soul

Initiate 13
A evolved soul that has mastered a lesson and earned admittance into a higher mystical order.

Inner Power 86
Soul force, Psychic force. Love force.

Inorganic beings / entities 47, 70, 82, 106
Fragmented soul particles that hang around in the lower astral planes. EGO energy balls without a physical or etheric form that hang around in order to merge with embodied souls.

Intent 129
An strong projected willpower towards a goal (that is for the good of all) in order to see it through.

Intuitive knowledge 231
Knowledge from the soul. The ability to sense the truth of a given reality using gut instinct.

Intuitive/creative body 47
A layer of the soul force field that stores divine knowledge in order to manifest.

J

Judgement 219
The act of labelling or drawing conclusions or invalidating another soul or life experience.

K

Kaleidoscopic 118
   Multidimensional reflections of the same vision.
Karma 136
   Cause and effect manifestations seen from the fourth dimension so the soul can see a reflection of his or her consciousness manifestations while in an embodiment.
Key numbers 127
   Two or more digits.
Kinesthetic sense 204
   The awareness of energy that the body possesses by virtue of being in motion.
Kundalini energy 159
   Life force energy ascending up the spine from planet earth up and out of the crown chakra.

L

Language of Light 12, 13
   The language of the soul
Language of Light symbols 144
   Pictorial or symbolic images that reflect quality particles of energies from the soul that hold the creative force of the great spirit of all that is.
Lateral thinking 16
   An ability to solve problems by illogical means.
Life force 160
   Vital Life Force (spirit) is the 'driver' of the auric energy field of the soul. Without This Vital Life (spirit) there can be no Soul. Soul is an energy-expression of all our spiritual experiences.
Linear 244
   (1) Line drawings involving one dimension only. One line or only one way of thinking. (2) third-dimensional, measuring of past, present, future, horizontal time
Logical thinking mind 70
   A reasoning mind with the ability to chain ideas together.
Lower mental body 208
   Used by the EGO or the persona.

M

Magnetic 153
   Feminine yin force that attracts the electric Male energy. The receptive, passive aspect of Spirit.
Magneto-electric 153
   Magnets that produce high voltage of electric energy.

Maldek 82
   A planet that is controlled by the illuminati that travels within the asteroid belt between Mars and Jupiter. Many science fiction writers tap into their akashic records to extract information of the times that they destroyed themselves and their planet using laser and atomic weaponry about 500,000 years ago.
Mandala 130
   A symbolic circular pattern representing the universe.
Manifestation 109
   Bringing something into a physical, emotional or mental awareness for others to perceive.
Mature compassionate Soul Age 29, 30
   At this stage 20 to 30% of soul energy is embodied but personalities are still 70 to 80 % in control. These people are moving into the fourth stage.
Mental telepathy 44, 162
   Thought transference between souls that are close. A natural form of communication between souls who have awakened to their higher dimensional selves.
Mesoamerican times 20
   Ancient writing systems including: pictographic, ideographic, logographic, syllabic, and alphabetic scripts.
Multidimensional 190
   Expanded awareness. Being aware of many dimensions simultaneously.

N

Nirvana 26
Buddhist expression of Bliss Consciousness.

O

Observing mode 136
Stepping out of one's self to look back on our self.

Octave 100
Series of eight notes occupying the frequency of vibration of the other.

Octahedron 157
A solid figure contained by eight triangular faces.

Organic computer 204
The human brain.

Orphanage of Soulmates 70
Richard's journal: reprinted as The Astral Explorer and The Cosmic Traveller

Our Source 129
All that is, God, almighty, Supreme being.

Oversoul 82, 129
A collective entity comprised of many souls.
(2) POWAH the oversoul of the Jaarsma family tree.(see www.ascensiontopics.com)

P

Paradigm 98
A fundamental shift in reality in order to create a new reality.

Peaceful Bliss 62
A quality aspect of soul that will uplift human awareness about living towards one's dreams.

Perception 154
Capable of perceiving the intuitive recognition of a truth or an aesthetic quality.

Perseverance 62
A persistence and determination. A soul quality.

Pictorial symbols 14
Pictographs used to express a word or a idea or a feeling through a symbol rather than words.

Planetary beings 249
Mercury, Venus, Earth, Mars, Saturn, Jupiter, Pluto, Uranus, Chiron.

Platonic solids 157
Building blocks of physical matter.

Polarities, Law of 18
Anything that has a dualistic nature or a set of positive and negative poles

POWAH 70
Name for the Oversoul energy of the author

Psychic energy 109
Soul force.

Psychic feeling 200
A Higher awareness extra-sensory perception. Perceiving with the imaginative faculty of the mind.

Psychic feeling centres 42
The seven major energy vortexes called Chakras

Psychic hearing 220
See Clair audience.

Psychic intuitive centre 231
The third eye and the crown chakra.

Psychic power 19
Invisible force that can heal and release old beliefs and thought forms.

Q

Qualities 155
Energy gifts that benefit humanity as a whole in its evolution process.

R

Radio-active 153
A nuclear force that has become unstable. Distortion in Alpha and Beta wavelengths.

Rational mind 161
Externally orientated conscious awareness mind on a day to day basis.

Root number 127
Single digit, primary number.

S

Sacral Chakra 27
Energy vortex chakra that relates to our adrenal glands where most of our thoughts that deal with sensational or sexual issues from our past or future are stored.

Security issues 51
Stored in the Base/Root chakra

Solar Plexus 29
The master antenna chakra where the autonomic nervous system provides direct access and is linked to every major organ and most endocrine glands.

Soul 140
The energy field of Soul (also called aura, or an individual matrix.) holds the energy-expression of all our spiritual experiences. An etheric library. The aura holds our akashic records.

Soul awareness 156
The percentage of soul (psychic) energy that is embodied.

Soul consciousness 206
An consciousness awareness from the 5th and 6th dimensional level.

Soul linage 139
A soul family going way back to the beginning of creation.

Soul mate 116, 139
(1) Souls that cross your path in order to awaken the spirit within, (not necessarily belonging to your soul family). Souls you have a contract with to work out karma. Souls that belong to your soul family and you planned (before an incarnation) to join together to support each other to awaken to full consciousness. (2) See twin souls.

Soul passion 45
An energy that motivates and encourages the soul to embody more of itself through the physical form.

Soul Plane 248
The 5th and 6th dimension and higher.

Soul purpose 62, 129, 190
An activity or intent that will bring about full awakening.

Soul-force 116, 138
(1) Psychic energy force (2) Life force.
A mystic psychic energy force carrying with it the idea of power.

Soul's vehicle of consciousness 139
The human field, aura or matrix.

Source consciousness 244
All that is

Spirit 140
(1) Vital Life Force. The energy of the Godhead (2) Intelligent energy that permeates all of creation. The non-individualized aspect of soul.

Strands of DNA 26
DNA molecule. Thread or strip of DNA molecules twisted around each other to form a double helix.

Structure 74, 250
Quality of Soul.

Subconscious 162
A specific part of the mind that is beneath the surface of consciousness. It's a section that stores past experiences. Our memory data that is accessible at any time. It is a divided part of the mind that is responsible for the bodily functions such as heartbeat, body temperature, etc.

Subtle bodies 230
The etheric, emotional, mental and creative intuitive bodies. Layers of selective consciousness within the auric force field.

Supreme Creator 219
The Godhead of All That Is encompassing both polarities. There cannot be one without the other.

Synchronicity 23
Simultaneous occurrence of events which appear significantly related but have no discernible connection. The energy of synchronicity guides us to improve our preparation in order to manifest our desires.

T

Tarot 162
A set of cards that depict archetypes or primary aspects of life.

Tetrahedron 157
A four sided solid; a triangular based pyramid.

Third Eye Chakra 30
The sixth sense organ that is located in the middle of the forehead between the eyebrows. This energy vortex transmits thought-forms through the pituitary gland.

The observer 15
In modern physics the phenomena of the cosmos require an observer in order to be learned about and understood by us. In my website the articles about the observer means that each individual's observer is the soul's mirror, the part that reflects - The Intuitive Higher Self - never the Mental EGO script

The God gene 20
Human spirituality is not the same as religion. "Religion is transmitted primarily not by genes but by ideas that are passed on from one individual to another through writing, speech, ritual, and imitation.". Our spiritual faith is hardwired into our Genes. It is mainly the product of our genetic make-up, while religion is the product of environmental and cultural factors.

266 The Language of Light

The Matrix 21
A mathematical language, and these codes form an Intercellular substance.

The Mayan Calendar 20
Is a system of distinct calendars and almanacs used by the Mayan civilization of pre-Columbian Mesoamerica. Mayan writing uses a syllabary made up of glyphs rather than a pure alphabet, it's a mixed system of glyphs and glyph groups. The glyphs are pictures.

Though forms 19,95
Energy balls with a creative potential

Thought-pictures 16
Electro-magnetic imprints that we see as visions of objects or worlds that are formed by meditative thought projections.

Throat chakra 30,38
The fifth sense organ that is located in front of the neck near the voice box; the centre of your creative expression.

Twenty two cards 23
The spacings of the 22 cards on the electromagnetic grid line of the human body represent the genetic decoding formula that hold the blueprint for the initiate that has the intent to ascend.

Twin soul 139
The original counterpart, or other half of a soul that has fragmented into two individual souls. The magnetic will (female) and the electric(male) force is the counterpart of Spirit. Each soul has only one twin soul.

U

Unconscious 162
No awareness or the part of Self that is inaccessible in one's present state of consciousness.

Unity consciousness 30
Crown chakra awareness that leads to freedom from the 3rd dimension reality. (2)The awareness of or a connection to universal mind in order to have a broad overview of different realities.(3) Language of Light quality.

V

Vanishing Worlds 153
Annelies' journal on the third level of the awakening plot.

Verification stage 29
The fifth or action stage of a manifestation.

Virtual reality 249
An artificial reality like a computer-simulated model using HTLM codes that create a virtual reality effect on our screens.

Visionaries 138
Idealists who foresee great advances in the future of humanity. The gift inherent within the sixth ray is the gift of seeing all things, including one's dark side.

Vortex 100
A whirling or rotatory motion that approaches a pursuit. They run along the etheric grid lines of our planet or our etheric grid formation. They absorb energy balls of thought- forms in order to create a mass.(2) see chakra,energy,cosmic or psychic vortexes.

Vowels 127
The letters a, e,i,o, u and sometimes y.

W

Wavelength 140
A particular mode of thinking and communicating. (2) electric-magnetic radiation.

William Gray 158
Well known Qabalist and practitioner of High Magic. Author of Exorcising the Tree of Evil.

Yin or Yang.
Yang, the masculine positive pole of creation.
Yin, the feminine negative pole of creation.

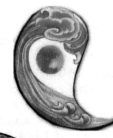

The LOGO of the ascension-journey

Bibliography.

Before this workbook was written for publication, I was inspired for many years by other authors who, like me, were searching for ways to awaken from the dream we call our reality. This Bibliography contains some of the fine books that will be of assistance to those that have chosen to follow the ascension journey. Not all the titles below deal with the ascension theory, but they have all influenced my life and the way I perceive evolution at the moment I'm typing this. You may not agree with everything that these authors have to say so read with discretion.

The Awareness of the Power of Words

Words like numbers and letters are energy pockets when they are combined.
Words represent the substance of pure energy.
Words have a vibrational essence which transcend and go beyond the interpreted meaning.
Words can bring into focus certain feelings and perceptions.
Words cannot only be isolated and created for the sole purpose of defining the immediate perception from the human perspective.
Words are much more than that and can help, assist, guide, and move our consciousness towards that which is Wordless, that which is limitless.
Words can only go so far, for words are used only to interpret, to label and to define.
Words must flow, so don't contain them.
Words must be what they are.
Words point the way but they can also get in the way.
Move beyond Words and feel the wordless meaning of that which is being presented.
Words are only stepping stones to truth.
Words can only serve as arrows pointing toward the Inner Truth,
Divine Self, the Real Self, the Higher Self, the Real You.
All of these concepts are simply Words that are attempting, from the human perspective, to describe that which is indescribable, which is infinite, which has no boundaries, which has no limits.
Words can only be a medium of exchange between souls that recognize the love and the light of Creation.

Taken from the novel: **The Awakening Clan**

Activation for Ascension
    David A. Ash, Kima Global Publishers, Cape Town, South Africa
A Course In Miracles
    Foundation for Inner Peace, Tiburon, CA
Ageless Body Timeless Mind.
    Deepak Chopra M.D, Harmony Books/ New York
Alchemy
    The evolution of the mysteries - Rudolf Steiner - Sophia Books
Astrology, Psychology and the four Elements.
    Stephen Arroyo, M.A., CRCS Publications CA

Autobiography of a Yogi
   Paramahansa Yogananda, Self-Realization Fellowship, Los Angeles, CA
Colour
   Rudolf Steiner, Rudolf Steiner Publications, Anthroposophic Press, New York
Colour healing
   Theo Gimbel, with Gaia Books Limited, London
Cosmic Memory
   Rudolf Steiner, Rudolf Steiner Publications, New York
Creating Mandalas.
   Susanne F. Fincher, Shambhala, Boston & London
Destiny of Souls.
   Michael Newton, Ph.D., Llewellyn Publications, USA
Drawing on the Right Side of the Brain
   Betty Edwards, A Jeremy P. Tarcher/ Putnam Book, G.P Putnam's Sons, New York
Earth, Air, Fire & Water.
   Scott Cunningham Llewellyn Publications, U.S.A
Exorcising the Tree of Evil
   William G Gray, Kima Global publishers, Cape Town, South Africa
Handbook to Higher Consciousness.
   Ken Keyes, Jr, Living Love Publications, USA
Knowledge of the Higher Worlds How is it achieved?
   Rudolf Steiner, Rudolf Steiner Press, Bristol
Life on the Cutting Edge
   Sal Rachele, Living Awareness Productions, Sedona AZ
Light Emerging
   Barbara Ann Brennan, Bantam Books, USA
Rising out of Chaos
   Simon Peter Fuller, Kima Global Publishers, Cape Town, South Africa
The Keys of Enoch
   J.J. Hurtak, Academy for Future Science, Los Gatos, CA
The Lost Realms
   Zecharia Sitchin, Avon books, New York
The Power of Silence
   Carlos Castaneda, Black Swan, London
The Power of Your Other Hand
   Lucia Capacchione, Ph.D. NewCastle Publishing CO., INC North Hollywood, CA
Theory of Colours.
   Johann Wolfgang von Goethe, The M.I.T Press, London
The Art of Dreaming
   Carlos Castaneda, Harper Collins Publishers London.
The Life and Teachings of the Masters of the Far East
   Baird Spalding, De Vorss & Co., Marina Del Rey, CA
The Gnosis and The Law
   Tellis S. Papastavro, Group Avatar, Tucson, AZ
The Holographic universe
Michael Talbot, HarperCollins Publishers, London

About the Author

Nadine was born in Holland, became a nurse, emigrated to Australia and then to South Africa which is still her home. She studied metaphysical sciences, esoteric psychology, art therapy, and gave drawing skill classes.

She also worked as a volunteer marriage guidance counsellor during the time this novel was written.

After her physic experience: hearing a voice that told her to expand her awareness during the seventies, Nadine felt a great urge to connect deeper with her soul. She spent a great amount of time reading and in committing herself to daily self-healing practices. Her psychic abilities opened so she had to learn to deal with all she could see, hear and feel. This awareness brought on lots of emotional sadness. Knowing what others think and feel is not always so wonderful.

In 1995, Nadine started to recognize her first Language of Light mind drawings. She began to draw mainly in the early mornings. She strongly felt that her hand was guided while each code type pattern was created. During the following years, day and night, her life was dominated by this task. While writing her first novel, by fictionally translating her feelings into a story telling format, her own life drastically changed. In 2000 she was shown the universal symbols in her workbook, that looked very similar to hers on page 30. She was encouraged to used them in her work, for they were universal symbols to be shared by all.

Nadine has been teaching many people, using a creative 'wholesome' process, for the past twenty years to create a bridge between our logical and intuitive abilities. She started to investigate the concept of awakening to full consciousness during the eighties. By combining many esoteric and scientific conclusion about this life in this third dimensional hologram, she developed an genetic decoding system that could be used in, what she called: The Awakening Game. Annelies' awakening workshop, which is the focus point of her first novel, takes the reader on a journey that could be their own.

Nadine held these genetic decoding trial workshops, which inspired her to write the concepts behind her theories in the form of Visionary Fiction, in order to reach others through story telling. Through her drawing skill classes she noticed the shift of her student's perceptions from the way that they looked at their drawings. When proof is shown, a belief becomes a knowing. As a result her Art-analogue mind-drawing workshops were born.

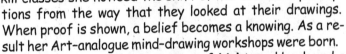

Together with **The Language of Light** workbook and a teachers manual, Nadine is still facilitating Art-analogue mind-drawing workshops for future facilitators who want to give mind-drawing classes throughout South Africa and abroad. These creative card making workshops will prepare her readers for their second workbook: **'The Body 'Codes of Light.'** written about in her novels **'The Awakening Clan - The Astral Explorer - The Cosmic Traveller and Vanishing Worlds.**

A4 drawing manual with all the exercises.

The Awakening series have the following purpose..

In Nadine's first romantic / visionary novel **The Awakening Clan** Ingrid, one of Annelies students, writes how her reality changes due to her own desire to awaken her soul purpose. Annelies' ascension-workshops teach a type of decoding exercise in order to activate the genetic cellular memory of her students.

The two following novels: **The Astral Explorer** and **The Cosmic Traveller**, Richard writes his own version on how Annelies' awakening card game titled: the **Eye of the observer** shows that our reality is a holographic third dimension game.

Vanishing Worlds, (not yet in print) is Annelies' journal. When the Crystal skull takes her on a macrocosmic journey, her internal dialogue with atomic level particles that make up her genetic body codes tell her a story how fantasy particles established the human identity.

The following awakening novels (not yet written) through Yolanda and the Eye of the Beholder, these journals will prepare the reader for their own ascension journey.
The Body Codes of Light - The decoding of your original blueprint
Is full of exercises that are backed up with a question and answer dialogue between Annelies and POWAH (the higher self 'guide' of the Jaarsma Clan). The workbook takes the reader on a journey, like the journey Annelies' students write about. Together with the Language of Light workbook, an idea starts to emerge that could have fooled the most brilliant scientist.

The Awakening Clan -Ingrid's first journal

By Nadine May

FORECASTING A POSSIBLE FUTURE FROM THE YEAR 2008 ONWARDS. WHERE WILL THE PROCESS OF SPIRITUAL TRANSFORMATION LEAD US?

This award-winning visionary novel takes readers into our near future where new-paradigm lifestyles result in the awesome possibility of reaching full consciousness that could even lead to physical ascension.

Darkest intrigue, basest treachery and the sweep of human destiny are set against a futuristic background that could be real.

This novel comes with a warning: it may forever change your world view.

ISBN 0-958435936

Available around the world and in all local bookstores in SA.

The Astral Explorer - Richard's first journal

Richard's journal takes the reader into different dimensions. Like **The Awakening Clan**, the theme on how the illusion of 'Time' can be an adventure if the reader is the observer, will prepare the reader for their own awakening process.

The main plot-driven theme on 'Time' takes the reader further into the often bizarre worlds within worlds. On the physical side Ingrid's story carries on and becomes Richard's story, but Richard carries the awakening plot into different realms. It's through the higher dimensions where the concept of 'Time' changes altogether, that makes this novel stand out from general fantasy novels.

Often 'fiction' can carry more truth that non fiction.

ISBN 978-0=9802561-6-1
Available around the world and in all local bookstores in SA.

The Cosmic Traveller - Richard's second journal

This third awakening novel completes Richard's journal when he is – BECOMING AWARE OF BEING UNAWARE

Ancient tunnels are exposed through an explosion under the construction site at the Valley of the Gods resort in France. Embedded in the rock walls are 'pictograms' that foretell a future that seems to have happened in the past. Richard learns on the astral plane that self-mastery cannot be expressed in words or pictures, but that it can awaken at great cost to our material reality.

During these chaotic times when the Outer Worlds (dark shadow forces) are busy robbing the planet of her valuable minerals, with the assistance of many human beings who are unwittingly infected by the virus called 'fear - or greed', the people who form the Jaarsma clan have to overcome their identify through learning how awaken their inner observer.

ISBN 978-09814117-0-5

Vanishing Worlds - Annelies' journal

Vanishing Worlds - Annelies' journal - LETTING GO OF THE OLD

Annelies' journal is riddled with magic from Hidden Worlds where our thought forms become real.

By now the Jaarsma Clan's group soul energy has to confront its own 'karma' in order to carry on the evolution path towards enlightenment. The individuals who are, 'on a soul level', belonging to the Jaarsma group-soul vibration, have a hard time adjusting to the new incoming paradigm. They have to stay in their 'observer mode' in order to identify their own often dark shadow companions.

Her awakened mastery of clairvoyance, telepathy and her ability to travel inter-dimensionally helped her to see how the visible worlds, created by emanations from the "Superior Beings," had all disappeared before. But there is hope for the human race.

Forth coming! in 2010

The Body Codes of Light - Decoding your original blueprint

This creative decoding workbook is an original, fun-filled, and thoroughly unique introduction to the sciences of letters, numbers and their role in creativity including absurd adventures that teeter on the edge of logic and astonishments.

By creating a body field map and dividing it into twenty two spacings, Nadine intuitively recognised how each layer or spacing formed a body field wave pattern. It was through translating these patterns into soul quality particles that the vibrations of these virtues affected her outlook on life.

How these symbols, that stood for the genetic codes can shed light on the mystery of our creation came as a surprise to her.

The origins of the Tarot, Astrology, I-Ching, Yoga, and her own graphic symbols, and how the Pyramids, were build by sound, all had one thing in common with her own decoding system.

We truly live in times when the great transformation shifts will bring about **Freedom**

Attention is not the only way we create in our lives, but it's an important part of our evolution.

Forthcoming! in 2010

Kima Global Publishers is an independent publishing company based in Cape Town.

We specialise in Books that Make a Difference to People's Lives.

- We have a unique variety of Body, Mind and Spirit titles that are distributed throughout South Africa, the U.K., Europe, Australia and the U.S.A.

- Among our titles you will find Non-Fiction, Healing, Esoterics, Philosophy, Parenting, Business coaching, Personal Development, Creative workbooks and Visionary Fiction.

- Kima Global Publishers helps to shape and groom new writers to become successful authors.

Robin Beck

CPSIA information can be obtained
at www.ICGtesting.com
Printed in the USA
FSHW020558141021
85472FS

9 780981 427850